Hear Now
A Way of Zen and Mindfulness

Zen Mister Series
Volume III

Zen Master Bub-In
Peter Taylor

Hear Now

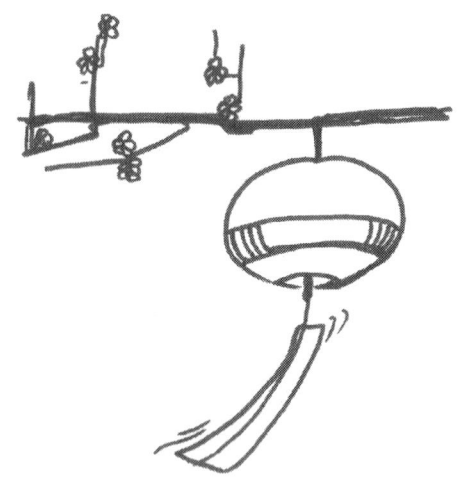

Contents

Introduction - *The Sound of Mindfulness* — vii

Chapter 1 - *Thinking and Suffering* — 1

    Back to School — 2
    Suffering Meter — 4
    Subtle Violence — 5
    That Voice — 7
    Just Thinking — 8
    Autopilot — 10
    Don't Know the Words — 12
    Broken Hearted — 14
    Enjoy Your Misery — 16

No Reason To Be Miserable	17
Free as a Bird	19
The Mindfield	20
Suffering Without Suffering	22
Easing and Ending Suffering	24
Heads Up	26
Emptiness	28

Chapter 2 - *Self and Ego* — 31

Full of Myself	32
Hey You	34
Assume You're Awesome	36
Identity Crisis	38
Water and Wave	39
When Things Hurt	40
Change Your Life	42
Unapologetic Ego	43
Compelling Drama	44
Big and Little Self	46
A Little Encouragement	47
Everything Is One	48
One Mind	49
Most Important	50
Self-Awareness	51
Self-Acceptance	53
Believe It	54

Chapter 3 - *Time and Space* — 55

Zen Moments	56

Mind Power	58
Time Travel	60
One Step	62
The Middle Path	64
Where You Are	65
Cosmic Accounting	67
Zen Hope	69
Everything Zen	70
A Way We Go	72
Not Feeling It?	73
Appearing and Disappearing	75
Clean Slate	76
When Will Life Get Easier?	78

Chapter 4 - *Meditation and Mindfulness*   81

The Purpose of Meditation	82
Applied Zen	84
Tips for Zen Practice	86
Low Motivation	87
Getting Annoyed	88
Getting Angry	90
Meditate	92
Finding Balance	93
Steppingstones	94
Stories, Feelings, and Compassion	95
Ugly Shoes	97
Moody Weather	98
Mood Matters	100

Anxiety Awareness	101
Controlling Emotions	103
Letting Go	105
Good and Bad	107
A Positive Light	108
Finding Your Happiness	110
Happiness Happens	112
No Complaints	113
Common Sense	115
Kissing Boo-Boos	117

Chapter 5 - *Love and Enlightenment* — 119

Being Enlightened	120
The Path of Peace	122
The Five Desires	123
The Antidote	125
That's That	126
Alright not All Right	127
Mind Tricks	128
Delusion	130
As It Is	131
Nothing Matters	133
Why Bother?	134
Helping Others	136
Other People's Minds	138
Spiritual Envy	140
Tea Party	141
Dream On	142

Life and Grief	144
Wondrous World	147

About the Author　　149
About the Artist　　150
About Inroads Press　　150

Introduction

The Sound of Mindfulness

Welcome home. You are here, now. This is where you live. Before you read any further, stop, take a breath, and listen to the sounds around you. What do you hear? That is the sound of mindfulness. That's pretty much it, nothing to it.

The beauty of mindfulness is that it is so simple. The difficulty of mindfulness is that it is too simple. It doesn't make sense that checking in with your senses can bring about peace of mind, but it can. All day and night the world bombards our senses with stimuli. In order to get anything done, we have to actively ignore everything that we don't need. All of that ignoring lulls us to sleep. Purposefully checking in with our senses wakes us up again.

There is a difference between mindfulness and just listening. Mindfulness includes an attitude of acceptance. It contains a recognition that something special is going on. To approximate the attitude of mindfulness, pretend that there is a great party going on in your house and you were not invited. It's your party, it's for you, and all of your friends are there. You even arranged the party, but you forgot to invite yourself. You find yourself sitting upstairs, feeling lonely, and becoming increasingly annoyed at the noise from all the merriment going on beneath you. Listening is just hearing the noise. Being mindful is transforming your discontent by crashing the party.

Mindfulness is rooted in the present moment. It is an understanding that the party is always going on and you are either there or you want to be there. Although the party is the only place to be, it is nothing special. Sometimes it is painful, other times it is joyful, but the pain at the party is tolerable. The pain of not being at the party is excruciating. When you are at the party, you have control. You can turn the music up, down, or off. You can decide when to dance and when to rest. You can even cry if you want to. You are there. You are in life's special place, now.

The idea that the act of centering yourself in present moment has the power to transform your life is appealing, but dubious. That is where Zen comes in. Zen is the Buddhist tradition of mindfulness and meditation. Zen has long tradition, dating back the Buddha, of exploring the nuances of the present moment to come to a deeper understanding of life. It represents the faith that it is possible to transform and transcend suffering. Zen provides faith and, at the same time, encourages practitioners not to rely on faith, but to experience the transcendence for themselves. Then it goes about trying to trick the practitioner into letting go of all the mental blocks that stand in the way of that experience.

Zen challenges people to see for themselves what is really going on. It gives clues about where and how to look. Look at yourself. Look with compassion, without judgment. Look with all of your senses. In Buddhism, the senses include the five senses of taste, touch, smell, sound, and sight and also includes a sixth sense of thought.

The senses represent a purity of the present moment through which your attention interacts with the greater world. Your senses are your trusted friends that remain true, beyond any concepts you use to embellish them. The act of meditation and the attitude of mindfulness is how you stick by your trusted friends and let them show you the way. Meditation is just sitting still and being aware of the activity of your mind. It is seated mindfulness. Mindfulness is checking in with the present moment as we go about our busy lives, it is walking meditation.

This book is a cheerleader for Zen and mindfulness. It cheers for the process so that you might give it a try to see if it works for you, and it might. The title of the book, *Hear Now*, is both a play on words pointing to a marker in time and space, the here and now, and an instruction to turn to your senses and engage in the present moment. The chapter names are subliminal messages placed on alternating pages to highlight the message of the text. *Thinking and Suffering* reminds you of a strong link between those activities. *Self and Ego* reminds you of the important difference between those concepts. *Time and Space* is another reminder of the vastness of experience that can always be reduced to the here and now. *Meditation and Mindfulness* is more rah, rah, rah for the way to salvation. Finally, *Love and Enlightenment*, like the first chapter is meant to draw a connection between love, which you understand, and enlightenment, which can mean almost anything.

    The best way to experience the wisdom of this book is to sit on it and meditate. The second best way is to smack it against a table and hear the sound of mindfulness. If those don't work for you, please read it.

Chapter 1

Thinking and Suffering

Back to School

If you've ever suffered in school, then you know what it's like to be involved in a painful learning process. To transform and transcend your suffering with mindfulness, go back to school.

In learning to transform suffering, school comes to you. Instead of suffering through long-winded lectures from self-important bores, suffering itself becomes the teacher. You become the self-important bore.

When you notice yourself suffering, school is in session. To learn from suffering, remember your ABC's: Awareness, Breathing, and Compassion.

When you notice the onset of suffering, become aware. Take a deep breath and give a long exhale. Engage your compassion and greet your teacher with respect. *Good morning, Suffering*. Don't secretly wish for it to go away. Hold it in your compassionate awareness and breathe. Remind yourself that you don't want to suffer, you don't deserve to suffer and you don't need to suffer. That is the essence of compassion. When you see your suffering through compassionate awareness, it becomes something separate from you. You can ask it questions and learn from it.

Don't question the story of suffering; question the feeling. If you think you are suffering because your parents were insensitive, that may be. That is the story, but don't think about that, think about how it feels to suffer. Breathe in. Pay attention to the teacher. Breathe out. When you are less actively suffering, you can explore the stories.

When you pay attention to your suffering, you will acquire wisdom. If you stay with your teacher through each painful lesson, the lessons will become less painful. Eventually, it will be time for recess, then, time to go home, then, summer vacation and soon, you will graduate.

Study with patience and persistence. With this kind of mindfulness, you will transform your life.

Suffering Meter

One way to gain an understanding of your suffering is to install a suffering meter in your mind. As gauging suffering is not exact, a suffering meter can be a rough instrument. The most important thing about a suffering meter is not how precise it is, but how often you check it. Your suffering meter only needs to have a positive, neutral, and negative value. For example: suffering, nothing, and contented, or miserable, neutral, and joyful, or 1, 0, and -1. Simple.

Every time you check your suffering meter, also check your thinking and figure out just what you were thinking that inspired the reading on your suffering meter. That way, you will see the connection between your thinking and your suffering.

The more often you check your suffering meter and check in with your thoughts, the more likely you will catch yourself thinking up reasons to suffer. If you just watch your meter all the time, you may recognize the cause of your suffering and see the way out.

You can also use your suffering meter on others. When you notice somebody else is suffering, as they often are, offer them compassion and kindness. See what that does to your own suffering.

Subtle Violence

Violence comes in many forms. It is not always loud and physical. Much of the violence we encounter in our lives, we do to ourselves, quietly behind the scenes. We silently think thoughts to ourselves that tell us we are not good enough, smart enough, strong enough, or capable enough. We think these violent thoughts so subtly that we don't notice we are thinking them at all. We just think our thoughts are the way things are. This subtle thinking violence can lead to all kinds of other violence when we act on our thoughts.

In order to stop this violent streak in your thinking, you have to catch the thoughts in progress. If you are feeling overly sad, anxious or angry, or if you find yourself hating yourself or others, you have violent thoughts running through your mind. To prove that you are entertaining these violent thoughts, watch your mind.

As you go about your day, notice yourself passing judgment. You may catch yourself thinking that other people are stupid, annoying, or ugly. If you notice yourself thinking those things about others, you will probably have similar fears about yourself. As you pay attention to your thoughts, you will notice yourself judging your own appearance or minor mistakes you make as though they were big problems. When you catch yourself thinking these thoughts, whether they are directed at yourself or others, recognize them as violence, take a deep breath and dismiss them. As you get more practice noticing the violence in your thoughts, your thoughts will change.

Whenever you notice a violent thought, you can counteract the violence with a kind or compassionate thought. When you get good at addressing the violence in your thinking, you will not act upon the violence with your words or deeds. When you introduce more compassion to your thoughts, you will act out the kindness and you will feel happiness.

That Voice

What is that voice in your head? How does the voice in your head spill out of your mouth or onto the page? How does it change when you fall asleep? How does that voice interpret the world for you? How does is affect your moods? How do you control it? How does it control you? How is it you? How is it not you? How does it stop? What is beyond the voice? What is that voice?

That voice is our constant companion. Sometimes we are aware of it. Sometimes we are not. Sometimes it seems like we can control it because we can choose what we do. Sometimes it seems like we can't control it because it keeps us up at night when we want to sleep, or it prompts us to do things that we know are bad for us or others. Being aware of it is likely as close as we can come to being in control of it. Because that voice is a part of us, becoming comfortable with it is important.

Ideas that you have about that voice in your head and how that relates to life are more of that voice. As you read this, that voice both aligns with these words and judges these words. Words can't tell you how to relate to the voice, you need to see for yourself. That voice may not even be in your head. See what it is.

Just Thinking

Our minds go to some crazy places and take our bodies with them. Just like we can use our minds to control our bodies, we can use our bodies to control our minds. We can exhaust our bodies so our minds shut off. We can also shut off our minds to let our bodies either do the work they need to do, or get the rest they need. What do we do though when our minds don't shut off? What do we do when our minds wake us up at three in the morning? What do we do when our minds take us to the dark places and our bodies can't seem to do anything about it? When that happens, we can remind ourselves that wherever our minds take us is just thinking.

Anything that we think, no matter how real it may be, is just thinking. We may think up the cure to cancer, which would be exciting, but that is just thinking. We may think that life is too painful and purposeless, but that too is just thinking. If you think up the cure for cancer, write it down and share it. If you think that life is miserable, write it down and throw it out, or just throw it out. That is just thinking.

When you recognize that all of your thoughts and ideas about the world are just thinking, you find a little bit of freedom from your thoughts. When you recognize that you are not a clairvoyant prophet, your thoughts become a little easier to let go.

An overactive, worrying mind can be annoying. You can use your body to assist you in settling your mind. With meditation, you sit with your body absolutely still and focus all of your attention on your breath. Hold your hands still in your lap. Hold your tongue still on the roof of your mouth. Keep your back still and straight. Keep your eyes still and lightly focused on the floor in front of you. Rest your attention on your breath as it flows into and out of your lungs. As your mind tries to get away again, see that it is thinking and let the thoughts go. Come back to your breath.

When you learn to use your body to still your mind, you can use that skill to stop your thinking wherever you are. You can use your ears, to hear a sound to remind you that you are just thinking. You can use your nose to notice a smell. You can use your tongue to notice a taste. You can use your feet as you pay attention to each step. You can even recognize a thought to remind you that you are just thinking. Breathe. You're in control.

Autopilot

We are creatures of habit. Our habits are our homes. Much of our life is spent on autopilot. We have our morning routines and our bedtime routines. We are morning people or night owls. For babies and children, creating regular routines gives life a sense of predictability and comfort. Their bodies learn that when they put on pajamas, brush their teeth, hear a story and get a kiss, it's time to fall asleep. They slide down a predictable ramp into their dreams.

As we get older, we create habits for ourselves to help us make the millions of transitions we make everyday. We transition from asleep to awake, from upstairs to downstairs, from home to work, from hungry to full, from happy to sad, from alone to with others, from one thought to the next, from morning to night. Our habits carry us through all these transitions, reminding us how we deal with each situation so we don't have to think about it each time. Our habits that brought us comfort as babies sometimes fail to bring us comfort as we age. When that happens, we need to adjust our autopilots.

When our habitual thoughts and feelings take a wrong turn and we fall into a pattern of depression, anxiety or anger, we need to turn off our autopilots for a while and steer ourselves. This is not always easy, because our autopilots kick in on their own, bringing up habitual feelings in response to constantly changing circumstances. The feelings come along with habitual thoughts to justify their existence.

If you habitually worry, you have to ride your autopilot like a bull. Each time you feel the worry respond to your circumstance, acknowledge and examine the worry. Try not to get thrown by it. Compare your immediate concern to the great suffering of humanity and throw it on the pile. Take a breath, and grab the reins.

If your 3 am habit is to wake up with a fear of the day ahead, your body is in the habit of producing fear at that time. Check your autopilot and observe the thoughts that rush in to explain the fear. It's just a little more suffering for the pile. Breathe and watch the thoughts and feelings. Then rebuild that comforting ramp back into your dreams.

Don't Know the Words

Words contain our experience. They give us a sense of control. They put a lamp around our genie. They help us navigate the world as we know it and provide an island of comfort amidst the discomfort of the unknown.

Thinking is mostly done in words. We see a rose and we think, *that is a rose*. It becomes a word, something other than it is. We have contained it. We have defined it. We think we know it. Then we smell it and it is much more. We don't know anymore. If we don't have the words to describe how the rose smells, we just think *good* or *bad*. We can't stop the words. We can't stop the thinking. We can't help running to the comfortable island of what we know.

When we become uncomfortable with what we know, our words and our thinking have turned against us. Suddenly, there is nowhere to run for comfort. At that point, we can either stay on our safe island of what we know and continue to suffer from our doubts and worries, or we can step out into what we don't know and seek comfort there. Words will inspire us to take that step, and words will help us to find comfort. Instead of thinking, *good* or *bad*, we will think *what*? Instead of thinking, *I feel awful because this is terrible*, we will wonder, *what is this feeling, what is going on?*

Thinking and Suffering

When we step into the unknown, we will notice that we were always there. What we thought we knew was a lot of pretty words and ideas. There was never an island. There was never a lamp. The genie was always free.

Broken Hearted

There is no way to think your way out of a broken heart. A broken heart severely compromises the mind. Your heart becomes a drain and the whirlpool of your thoughts continually swirls down the hole. You stand by, helplessly, watching all of your plans, hopes, dreams, and self go round and round and down into oblivion. Any logical thought of how things will be fine in time just get sucked into the roiling waters and consumed by the abyss. The thoughts that pour from your mind are like fuses to emotional bombs that go off and fill you with anger, doubt, sadness, despair, and numbness. Each bomb is equally devastating. While all that is going on, you have to go about your life.

As you go about life with a broken heart, you are not entirely in control. You may not be able to stop the thoughts, which will churn in repetitive tedium. You may not be able to defuse the bombs, which are detonated by the uncontrolled thoughts. You may not even be able to control how you go about your life. Things that need doing may remain undone. Things that shouldn't be done are done.

You are also not entirely helpless. You can observe the mayhem. As you go about your life, recognize each emotion as it fills you. You can wash your dishes as you feel sad. You can mow the lawn as you feel angry. You can observe what bombs are attached to which thoughts. You can notice your thoughts go from blame to shame and down the drain. You can feel compassion for yourself, with or without feeling sorry for yourself.

When you live with a broken heart, you are forced into a certain amount of mindfulness. Your mind is full of large thoughts and there is no way to see around them. By using the imposed mindfulness of heartbreak to practice willful mindfulness, you develop skills to handle the rest of life's endless surprises.

Enjoy Your Misery

It is impossible to enjoy your misery. Enjoyment and misery can only jockey for position in your mind. They compete for your attention like a brother and sister pulling a parent in different directions. Like sibling rivals, enjoyment and misery can coexist. When you are feeling miserable, you can still enjoy a warm cup of tea, or a friendly smile. When you are enjoying a stroll in the park, you can still feel an underlying sense of doom and gloom. Actually enjoying a feeling of misery cannot be done.

The closest you can come to enjoying your misery is to acknowledge your misery. When you see that you are feeling miserable, don't demand happiness of yourself, but also don't wallow in misery. Wallowing is projecting your misery far into the future, without imagining the possibility of ever enjoying anything. You only need to give your misery its time. Take it in like bad poetry. Feel the discomfort. Listen to the story. Cry.

When you walk that line between allowing and wallowing in your feelings, you create space for peace. In the midst of a deep cry, there is peace. In recognizing that misery is a passing feeling and not a permanent state of affairs, there is peace. Although you cannot enjoy misery, because misery is miserable, within your misery, you can find peace. Peace is always enjoyable.

No Reason To Be Miserable

There is no reason to be miserable. Misery creates its own reasons and we just believe them. It is difficult to reason our way out of misery. In order to get out of misery, we have to stop reasoning and pay attention to our reasons for being miserable. When we are prone to misery, there is always a reason. Pain, suffering, sickness, fear, stress, rudeness, rain, sleet, cold, heat, noise, dark, odors, loneliness, work, school, hunger, boredom, anger, need, fatigue, doubt, and want can all be reasons to be miserable. These things are not really reasons to be miserable, they are just experiences we have. When we are prone to misery, these experiences may seem to cause our misery.

We find our way through the world by figuring out what we like and don't like. We try to create conditions that we like, but when we encounter conditions we don't like, we find it reasonable to become miserable. As we find ourselves becoming miserable, we find people to commiserate with us. We whine, gripe, and complain and our friends agree that we are completely justified in being miserable, considering what we are going through.

It is important to pay attention to your reasons for being miserable. Pay attention to your complaints. Pay attention to your experiences. When you question each experience and wonder if it is really a good reason to be miserable, you will expose your miserable habits. Once you start to notice all the little misery traps out there, you will learn not to step into them. If you feel the winter wind blow and you think the wind is making you miserable, feel the wind again. You may notice that the wind is reminding you that you are alive. That is a reason to rejoice.

Free as a Bird

The demands of life can be overwhelming. When life demands that we be a certain way and we are not that way, the unfair demands drive us to despair. If life's demands seem impossible, we don't need to despair. We need to change how we think about life. We need to think like the birds.

Life is not demanding. We are demanding of life and of ourselves. Birds don't get up in the morning and curse the fact that they need to sing and get worms. They get up, sing and get worms. Life mostly demands that we get up, get worms and sing. All of the extra demands have to do with our style, with our ego.

We trouble ourselves endlessly with what kind of worms we get, where we eat those worms, and where we'll find the next worm. We worry about singing. We have an endless variety of songs to sing. We want to sing the right song and sing it perfectly. We want people to love our song. We want people to recognize us in our song and love us. It can be hard to sing when so much is riding on the song.

When life becomes too demanding, don't despair. Fly. Have a worm. Sing your song. That's all that life demands. Be as free as a bird. Tweet, tweet, slurp, chirp, chirp, chireeee.

The Mindfield

If you are feeling overwhelmed with life, it is hard to know were to begin to address the problem. If you go to a psychologist or a counselor, they can help you look at your life and break it down into little pieces that are not so overwhelming. You can learn to dismantle huge, daunting tasks into small manageable pieces and then figure out which things you need to to first. A psychologist can help you look at your life and divide it into those beliefs, behaviors and relationships that are helpful to you and those that are harmful. They can help you learn to tiptoe through your triggers in the minefield of your mind. With this approach, you gain a sense of control and the confidence that you can cope.

If you are feeling overwhelmed with life and you turn to a Zen Master, they will tell you to throw out your mind. Instead of learning to identify which parts of you are good and which are bad, you will break down the barriers that appear to separate you from the ground beneath you and the sky above. With this approach, you give up all hope of control and gain the confidence that you can cope anyway.

Life comes as a whole and in pieces. Sometimes it is necessary to deal with the pieces, but it is helpful to be aware of the whole. When you think about your whole life, with all the ups and downs, heartbreaks and triumphs, you feel a sense of gratitude for the richness of your experience.

Your experience today is not just tasks, chores and events, it is your whole life. If that seems overwhelming, focus on the task of breathing. That is also your whole life, but it seems manageable. However you view your life, you are both a part of everything and apart from everything. Whichever way you turn, you can cope.

Suffering Without Suffering

There is suffering and there is suffering. There are all sorts of situations where we suffer. We suffer when we're tired, cold, bored, angry, hot, sad, scared, hurt, hungry, lonely, in pain, stressed, annoyed or just basically discontented. There are hundreds of ways to suffer. It is possible to experience these feelings without actually suffering. We suffer when we resist these feelings. We suffer when we give in to these feelings. We suffer when we get carried away with these feelings. To stop suffering through suffering, pay attention to your suffering and pay attention to suffering from your suffering.

People learn to live with suffering. If you look at a professional football player you may wonder what kind of fool would go out on that field knowing that they will be pummeled by 300 pound men trained in inflicting pain. The players learn to suffer without suffering. They become adept at dealing with physical pain. As you notice your various ways of suffering, you will be able to experience the suffering without suffering so much.

A good way to notice suffering is in the shower. As the water temperature changes you begin to suffer. You quickly adjust the temperature. That little tiny suffering you endure before you adjust the temperature gives you an opportunity to observe your suffering. If you run out of hot water, notice how your suffering from cold turns into suffering from anger at the person who showered before you.

    When you practice noticing your suffering you see how you lean into or pull away from your discomfort. You notice that you are able to manage the feeling. You notice how the feeling feels. When you get good at observing your suffering, you will find yourself suffering without suffering. When you can do that, you'll also notice yourself not suffering at all. You'll notice yourself feeling good.

Easing and Ending Suffering

To end your suffering, practice mindfulness constantly. To ease your suffering, practice mindfulness occasionally. Most people don't believe that it is even possible to end their suffering, so they engage in practice to ease their suffering. Easing suffering is good too. When you suffer a lot, a break is nice. When your goal is to ease your suffering, you can do that by satisfying your wants. If you're tired, take a nap. If you're lonely, find a friend. If you're bored, do something. If you just need a break, take a break. It can be easy to ease suffering.

To end suffering you have to believe that it is possible to end suffering, then remain vigilant in your awareness of your suffering, so that you can see its cause. Pay attention to your wants. Don't just give in to your desires, but see what they are about and see how they contribute to your suffering.

Pay attention to your mind. If it is possible to end suffering by changing the way you think, then watch your mind closely to see how you think.

Also, pay attention to yourself. If it is you that is suffering, you have to figure out just what you are. You have to determine what you want from yourself, what you think about yourself and what it is in you that suffers. That inquiry is a life long project, but if you pursue it wholeheartedly, somewhere along the way, your suffering may stop.

Thinking and Suffering

Whether you seek to ease or end your suffering depends on your faith. If you think it is possible to end your suffering, you will take one path. If you think it is only possible to ease suffering, you will take another path. They may be the same path, but your belief will determine how much you suffer as you travel.

Heads Up

If you want to clue somebody into something that is happening, you give them the heads up. If you think that somebody is clueless, you may say that they have their head up their ass. If you think that somebody has their head up their ass, you may want to give them the heads up. That is the Buddha's message in a nutshell. Heads up.

If your head were really up your ass, you would have a unique perspective of yourself. You would also suffer. If somebody pointed out to you that your head was stuck up your ass, you probably wouldn't believe them and you may become angry. Two symptoms of having your head up your ass are not knowing exactly where your head is, and becoming easily angered. If somebody told you that the way to end your suffering was to take your head out of your ass, and you began to entertain the idea that your head may actually be up your ass, then you would probably do all you could to change your head space.

The Buddha's message is more compassionate and less vulgar, but it is essentially a heads up to the idea that there is a way to end your suffering. One of the roots of suffering is a sense of a separate self. If you see the world with your head up your ass and you recognize where your head is, then you will also realize that everything you see is you. When you notice that all you are seeing is

Thinking and Suffering

yourself, you no longer feel so separate from it and your suffering stops.

Your head is always up to something that causes you to suffer. Whenever you notice that you're suffering, just give yourself the heads up and realize that your ass is perfect.

Emptiness

Where in the world do we find emptiness? If you feel emptiness in your heart, is that emptiness or something else? If you feel lonely, you are empty of the kind of love you imagine, or empty of the company you desire. If you are unfulfilled, you are empty of satisfaction. If you feel worthless, you are empty of self-esteem. You are not empty. You are full of ideas. You are full of pain. Emptiness is not good or bad. It is relative.

If you have a bucket of water, it is heavy. If you pour out the water, the bucket becomes light, empty of water, full of air. Your mind is like the bucket, full of ideas and feeling heavy. Ironically, that heaviness is associated with emptiness. These are our values. We think heavy and empty are bad. Light and full are good. No wonder it's hard to be happy.

If your heart feels heavy and empty, then you are feasting on thoughts. Your heart is full of flesh and blood. It weighs less than a pound. It is neither heavy nor empty. Thoughts have no weight. They are energy. Yet they feel massive. Your thoughts are concerned with good and bad, pretty and ugly, right and wrong, self and other, heavy and light, full and empty. This kind of thinking leads to heartache.

When you notice an empty feeling in your heart, then try to empty your head. By just watching your mind, you can change what goes on in it. When you embrace your emptiness, the weight of the world will no longer rest on you. When you become empty of your self, you become the universe. That's quite heavy.

Chapter 2

Self and Ego

Full of Myself

Like a glass is full of water, I am full of myself. This body that I walk around in is filled to overflowing with me. I am so full of me, that everything I do is tainted with me. I can't see you except through me. I can only taste food as it tastes to me. I can't imagine a world without me. As soon as I start to imagine, there I am, imagining.

For all of that me in me, I don't even know what it is that I am. This self that I am full of is made of things I don't understand. There is a body that contains a life force that sustains itself on food, water, air and love. I don't know If I am that body or that life force, or if I am something aware of that body and life force. I don't know for certain if that awareness is a combination of the body and life force or apart from it.

That self that fills me seems to have things to do beyond obtaining food, air, water and love. It has feelings and opinions and opinions about feelings. My self judges me and places a value on me by comparing an idea of me with an idea of what I should be or could be. Depending on the feelings that I feel or the ideas that pass through me, my value will go up or down. If my value goes to high, people will say I am full of myself. If my value goes too low, people will say I struggle with self-esteem.

If I don't even know what my self is, how can I place a value on it? If I go ahead and place a value

Self and Ego

anyway, how could that value be accurate? My self may be some only consciousness without mass. It may be the entire massive universe peeking through the goggles of my eyeballs. I can't tell whether my self is finite or infinite. That large a margin of error makes the idea of self almost empty of meaning. I may be full of emptiness, empty of myself, or full of myself.

    Have some tea.

Hey You

What you think of as yourself is just you. You don't have to think about what you are because it is so obvious. Everybody you know recognizes you when they see you. They call you by name. If somebody doesn't know your name they may just call you, *hey you*. You know that is you. You are you.

What you are to you, to your mother, to your best friend, to your worst enemy and to a stranger are all different. Who is right?

You are right. You know you best. You are with you all day and night. You know your every hope and fear. You know your dreams. You are privy to your inner most thoughts. Surely you must know you best. If you are the one who knows you best then you must love you the most.

If you don't love you the most, then perhaps your mother knows you best, because she loves you the most. Your mother knew you before you knew you, and she loves you with her soul. How could anybody who loves you so much not know you best?

Your best friend gets you. You can be yourself with your best friend and they love you for it. They accept you just as you are. Your best friend may know you best.

Self and Ego

You're worst enemy doesn't know you. They are shut down to you. They don't know squat. They have a distorted view of you. What do they know?

Strangers don't know you either. They see you and forget you, but it still matters what they see in you. You are something special. Even a stranger should be able to notice that.

What you are by yourself, with your mother, your best friend, your worst enemy and strangers are all different. Yet you are you. You are the same. So what is it exactly that you are? Who knows?

Assume You're Awesome

Take a moment and think about what you are. Think deeply about what you know about yourself. Think about how you fit in with the world. Think about why you were born. Think about what you were before you were born. Think about all the amazing things you've accomplished that bring you great pride. Think about all the things you've done that you wish you could have back, those things that cause you great shame. Think about how much of your life is within your control. Think about how much of your life is beyond your control. Think about things that have happened to you that are completely unfair. Think about privileges that you have that other's don't. Think about privileges that others have that you don't. Think about all the things you've worked hard for and you have because you deserve them. Think about all the things that have been given to you trough no effort on your part. Think about all the hardships you have endured because of things you have done. Think about all the hardships that have befallen you, which had nothing to do with what you have done. Think about your ability to think about you. Think about your body. Think about your breath. Breathe.

You are kind of complicated. Life is kind of complicated. It is difficult to know exactly what is right and what is wrong. It is hard to know what is good and bad. It is hard to know where you fit into the world. When you think about what you are, you think about your past actions, your family, your friends, what you do. You think about your body, its outward appearance, its inward functioning, its thinking, your thinking, your breathing. When you breathe, the oxygen in the air goes into you and the carbon in your body goes out. The number of trees and cars and factories in your neighborhood affects the quality of the air that becomes you. When you think about what you are, it's hard to know where you stop and not-you begins.

When you take a moment to think about what you are, you immediately know that you are you. When you think deeply about what you are, you stop knowing so much. There is a lot going on that makes up you. All that going-on is a spectacular event, constantly changing. Energy transforms into mass and mass into energy, not only in the middle of the sun and stars, but in the cells of your body. When you think about what you are, and what you do, you may gravitate toward feelings of guilt and shame, and somehow imagine that you are not what you should be. It's complicated to figure out what you are. Until you know, you should assume you're awesome. The evidence is all around you.

Identity Crisis

One aim of a Zen practice is to create an identity crisis for yourself. If you are already having an identity crisis, you are well on your way. The purpose of the identity crisis is to change your idea about who and what you are. This is an especially compelling idea if you are not content with who or what you seem to be now.

To create an identity crisis for yourself, throw out your idea of what you are. You may think that you are you, with all your problems, challenges, gifts and graces, but to create a crisis, you have to imagine that is not you. You have to entertain the idea that your idea of what you are is wrong.

If you manage to lose your idea of what you are, you will find yourself in an identity crisis. Then you will become obsessed with figuring out what you are. You will search for yourself like you have misplaced your car keys when you are late for work, or you can't find you cell phone. When you resolve that crisis and see what you are, you will be delighted. You will see then that you have always been that amazing thing that you are.

Water and Wave

To live peacefully with your emotions, don't worry about what you are based on what you feel. You can't stop feeling happy and sad, but you can stop hoping and fearing that each emotion will last forever.

You are a platform for emotions, an observer of emotions and emotions themselves. If you were a lake and your emotions were waves, no matter how wild your waves get, beneath the surface you are still a calm lake. The surface of the lake responds to the weather. Waves come up when the wind blows and abate when it stops. When the waves agitate the surface, the heart of the lake is at peace. When the wind stops, the lake clearly reflects the stars and the moon.

When you feel your life agitated with emotion, check the wind. Notice your breath and remember the calm at the heart of the lake. See what the waves are doing on the surface. See how your thoughts are the wind. When the wind stops, the waves abate. Don't worry about what you are. You are the water, the wind and the waves.

When Things Hurt

When things hurt, it is a good time to figure out who you are. The problem with figuring out who you are when things are hurting, is that you will likely be telling yourself all kinds of misleading stories about yourself. Don't believe everything you think. For example, if somebody betrayed you, you may think that you were stupid to trust that person. You may think that something in you invited the betrayal. You may think that you don't matter. Any kind of thought like that is the kind of thought you shouldn't believe. That kind of thinking is you adding to your betrayal by betraying yourself. To figure out who you really are, pay attention to your thoughts and notice if they are feeding your hurt or healing your hurt. When you start to notice misleading thoughts about yourself, you can see through them to whom you really are.

To see who you are pay attention to your feelings. If you are hurting, then you are somebody who hurts. That does not mean that you are weak or damaged. It means that you feel pain. It means that you deserve compassion and understanding. When you see that you deserve compassion and understanding, then you are beginning to see who you are. With that understanding, you begin to feel compassion for yourself.

When things hurt, you can see how brave and capable you are. When you focus on feeling what hurts and stop distracting yourself by criticizing yourself for getting hurt in the first place, you will see that you can manage even the most difficult situation. You will see how much courage you have as you face your pain directly. When you see how brave and capable you are, you gain faith that you will make it through your experience intact.

    You can't wish the hurt away, but you can watch it away. As you pay close attention to your experience, you will learn who you are, and you will like who you become.

Change Your Life

Like a loving parent changes a dirty diaper, you can change your life. If you think your life has soiled itself, it makes perfect sense to change it. As you go about changing your life, you do it in a spirit of compassion. Don't blame yourself for having created a mess. Take a look at the mess, peel it away, and throw it out.

You are a beautiful baby just going about your business. Your life story and your sense of yourself is like the diaper that fills up with all kinds of ideas about what you are and what you should be. When carried around too long, those ideas start to stink. That's when you know it's time for a change.

Changing your life does not have to involve a radical outward transformation. You don't need to shave your head and go live on a mountain. You just need to see yourself as a beautiful baby who deserves love and compassion. You can see everybody around you as babies too, many stuck in their own soiled selves. A baby's routine doesn't change with its diaper, it goes right back to doing its baby thing, only more comfortably.

You will need to change your life over and over again. Eventually, you will learn to use the potty and have no more use for your diaper.

Unapologetic Ego

Saying sorry is a good way to catch your ego doing its thing. The harder it is to say sorry, the easier it is to see your ego. Your ego is all that pain trying not to say sorry.

Children have a difficult time telling each other that they are sorry when they have done something on purpose. If they are angry, the last thing that they want to do is admit that they were wrong and try to make another person feel better. They become fully absorbed in their egos and have no empathy for the pain they have caused. If they are forced to apologize, they may say sorry in a way that inflicts additional pain.

Adults have similar struggles. Saying sorry can be an act of compassion. Saying sorry can be an act of humility. If your ego isn't all caught up in being humble and compassionate, saying sorry can challenge your ego. It becomes difficult to say. That is why it is a good practice to say sorry. It becomes extra good practice if you force yourself to say sorry and the other person tells you you should be. You can notice your ego as plain as the full moon when that happens.

Compelling Drama

When a movie, TV show, or play thoroughly entertains you, it is compelling drama. It sucks you right into the story. As you watch the action, you identify with the characters and live their lives and loves with them. When a drama is compelling enough, you disappear. When a movie is boring, your seat may become uncomfortable, you may get hungry, you may make comments to your friends, but when the story engages you completely, you are gone. There is only the story.

Your life is the most compelling drama there is. You were cast in the role of you and your only option is to play it brilliantly. Meryl Streep or Jonny Depp, could never play you with all the subtleties you put into the role. They are too busy being them (which probably isn't as easy as it looks). You play you with all your soul, with incredible attention to every little detail. When you stub your toe, you care immensely about the pain and you come up with inimitable facial expressions to demonstrate your inner experience. Unlike produced dramas, the role you play is not always filled with plot moving purpose. You have to keep playing you when you're bored, when you're cranky, when you're watching other dramas on television.

It is natural and unavoidable to be compelled by the drama of your own life. When big things are happening, it's easy to get sucked into the action.

The suffering that the drama creates is real suffering. It's different from suffering along with a movie character, because you have no confidence that it will end. It is also the same suffering. It's a different tune played on the same instrument, you.

When you are playing the role of yourself, no amount of suffering or joy will allow you to step out of character. Everywhere you step is still you. To relieve the suffering you can remember that you are acting. See what motivates your action. Marvel at your brilliance in creating an amazing, complex, unique human being. As you suffer, feel compassion for your character, for yourself. That's all part of the drama. It's completely compelling.

Big and Little Self

When you are concerned with your problems, your self is very big. When you are going about your life without thinking about anything, your self is little. If you see somebody drowning in a river and jump in to save them without thinking, you have no self at all. You are one with the drowning person.

A big self can be unwieldy. When your self is big, you have to worry about how you look, what people think of you and how you will survive in the world. You worry about success and failure. You wonder if you're good enough. When your self is big, it interferes with your enjoyment of life.

When you notice yourself lacking enjoyment in life, pay attention to what you are thinking and see how it relates to your self. You may be judging yourself, or judging others based on your idea of your self. As you practice noticing your self growing and shrinking, your self will remain a reasonable size. From time to time it will disappear as it merges with the world around you.

A Little Encouragement

You are wonderful. You are just as good as anybody else. Nobody else is any better than you. Think of the person you admire most in the world and you will understand just how wonderful you are. Think of a person who could really use some help and you will know how deserving you are. Think of the person you love most in the world and you will feel how much love is in you. There is never any need to compare yourself to others unless you find yourself doubting that you are something special. In that case, it could be helpful to give yourself a little encouragement by thinking about people who are special to you and reminding yourself that you are that special too.

Everything Is One

To see that everything is one does not take a great spiritual realization, it just takes a different approach to counting. You just look at everything and count to one. One. That's it. That's everything.

We are used to doing that with ourselves. We look at ourselves and we think, *this is me.* We know that we have eyes, ears and noses, but they are all parts of the one thing that is us. We like to look at ourselves and the world around us and count to two. This is me, that is not me. One, two. That's when things start to get complicated. That's when we start to worry about the part of the world that is us.

When we look at ourselves and the world and count to two, we try to grab things from the world to make them part of us. We grab people, things, and ideas. We get the idea that the part of the world that is us is inadequate, so we try to make ourselves better. There is nothing so wrong with us except how we count. When we think of ourselves and the universe and just count to one, we see that we are amazing.

One Mind

We all have minds that work kind of the same way. I have ideas and you have ideas. We both look at a rose and see a rose. We can pass ideas back and forth from one mind to another though words, music, facial expressions, gestures and semaphore.

Some people train their minds to feel happiness, others train their minds to cure diseases, still others train their minds to make music. All of these different mind specialties reinforce the impression that we each have only separate minds. We have developed property laws to protect our personal ideas. Yet all of our knowledge comes from ideas bouncing around between all of our minds.

There is little difference between an idea that comes to you as you sit and think and one that comes to you in conversation or from a book. Nonetheless, we take great pride or feel great shame in the ideas that pass through our personal minds.

When it gets cramped or lonely in your mind, or if you feel like your mind is working against you, you can turn to another's mind for a different perspective. Most other minds can see amazing things about you that you sometimes miss.

As ideas fill many minds, the rain makes many puddles and it makes the roses grow.

Most Important

Your life is the most important thing there is. What you do with your life is not so important. You have hopes and dreams for yourself, but trying to live up to those dreams takes you away from the most important thing there is, your life. There is no point in becoming something that you imagine you should be when you already are much more that you think you are.

You may have simple goals for yourself like trying to be nice, happy or mindful. You may have lofty goals like being president, curing cancer, or saving all sentient beings. You may just want to get through the day. You may do any or all of those things, or you may fail at any or all of those things. The most important thing is not that you succeed or even that you try, the most important thing is that you are alive. You are here. You are you.

Self-Awareness

Self-awareness is easy. If you notice you are hungry, then you are self-aware. If you notice you are tired, then you are self-aware. If you notice that you need to be more self-aware, then you are self-aware. Congratulations.

If self-awareness is so common, then what is so good about it? It's just being alive. That is good. If self-awareness is just being alive, then how can you become more self-aware? You can notice that you're hungry and have a snack. You can go to bed when you notice that you are tired. You can notice your experience of dissatisfaction with how things are and pay more attention to your life to make it more tolerable. That's not only being more self-aware, it is also being self-compassionate.

Self-compassion is good. Self-indulgent is not so good. Self-awareness is good. Self-consciousness is not so good. Is it possible to be compassionate to yourself without indulging yourself, or be aware of yourself without being conscious of yourself? Self-awareness is noticing how self-conscious you are. Self-awareness is noticing how you judge yourself, flip-flopping between good and bad. Self-awareness is noticing how compassionate you are to yourself.

As your self-awareness transforms into judgment-awareness and compassion-awareness, your view of yourself changes. As you practice consistently and compassionately, you become aware of some of your wonderful qualities. Soon you will become self-appreciative. You are no longer just being self-aware; you are actively building up to self-acceptance.

Self-awareness is good. Notice when you're hungry. Notice when you're tired. Notice when you're satisfied. Notice that you are noticing something all the time. Try not to worry about bad and good. Try not to worry about self. If you do worry, be aware, then be compassionate.

Self-Acceptance

Accepting yourself, as you are, does not mean being fine with your imperfection. It means accepting yourself as perfect, just as you are. If you are miserable, accept your miserable self. If you are happy, accept your happy self. It also means that if you are miserable, don't wish for your happy self. If you are happy, don't worry about your miserable self. If you find yourself being miserable and wishing to be happy, then that is how you accept yourself.

When you manage to accept yourself as you are, you will not likely find yourself miserable. Misery usually comes when you are wishing to be different from how you are. When you completely accept yourself, there is not much left to be miserable about.

Self-acceptance is not a compromise. It is a recognition, a realization. When you actually see just what you are, you will be delighted.

Believe It

It is important to believe that you are All That. It is not so helpful to try to prove it. You just need to believe it and move on. If you spend your time trying to prove that you are something special, you will never quite believe it, which means you will suspect that the opposite is true. You will end up creating tests. You will look for verification in things you achieve. You will seek affirmations from other people. You will look for confirmations in your moods. That is a dangerous game.

Although you may come up with 10,000 reasons why you are an amazing human being, just one stray idea to the contrary could convince you that you're mud. Unfortunately, it doesn't work as well the other way. If you come up with 10,000 reasons why you are worthless, one bit of evidence that you are spectacular will not convince you. That is, unless you absolutely believe it and then it's *game over*.

Once you believe that you are fantastic, just because you are, you no longer have to prove it to anybody, least of all to yourself. You become free to let your light shine on the world, showing others what a silly game we play.

You are All That. Believe it.

Chapter 3

Time and Space

Zen Moments

There are two ways to talk about Zen. One meaning of Zen is the Buddhist practice of sitting meditation and realizing our Original Nature. The other meaning of zen is a derivative of the first. It is a mellow, peaceful or contented state of mind. Certain times, when you feel connected to nature, absorbed in music, or appreciative of a particular quality of light can be considered zen moments. When people get all worked up over life events, they may imagine that they would be happier if they were a bit more zen about things. This popular meaning of zen associates it with acceptance and detachment as well as absorption in a fleeting experience. That is zen. The word has positive, almost Jedi, connotations.

If you aspire to have zen moments, it helps to have a Zen practice, which includes sitting in meditation. To meditate, sit, facing a wall and pay close attention to your breathing and stray thoughts. If you do this every day or a few times a day, then you have a dedicated Zen practice. If you want to deepen your practice, find a teacher and a meditation group. When you have a Zen practice, all of your moments are zen moments.

If you don't have a Zen practice, but every now and then you notice yourself experiencing the joy of life, or feeling quietly comfortable in the

Time and Space

midst of your misery, you may recognize those moments as zen moments.

Without a Zen practice, you may try to grab onto those zen moments. You may think that you are a better person in those moments than other moments. Even if you practice Zen, you may grasp onto those moments. That grasping is part of your practice. Those moments are wonderful and enticing. Who wouldn't try to grasp them?

Whether you practice Zen or not, you experience moments. To a Zen practitioner those are all zen moments. To a Jedi they are forceful moments. To a Christian they are Christian moments. To a Muslim they are Islamic moments. To a Jew they are Jewish moments. To an Atheist they are just moments. Moments have many faces, depending on who's experiencing them. Fortunately, you don't need to practice Zen to have zen moments. They are there for everybody, momentarily.

Mind Power

We think that we can't control things with our minds. That is the only way we can control things. We have amazing abilities to make breakfast appear on the table, flowers in vases, monkeys in space, all with our minds. Our minds make us get out of bed in the morning and dictate where our fingers go on the keyboard when we type. While our minds do these regular things they are also amusing themselves by travelling through time into a remembered past or an imagined future. As our minds facilitate travel through time and space, they also manufacture emotions to add depth and texture to the experience.

There is incredible creative power in our mind, but if we don't pay attention to what it is doing, it can create an uncomfortable, or uninhabitable, living space. Life is uncomfortable when it is experienced through opinions about what is wrong with the world and accompanied by the sense that nothing can be done about it. The mind that creates the discomfort has the power to fix it.

To gain some control of our mind, we need to see just what our mind creates and where it wanders. If it spends too much time in a better past or a scary future, it needs to be brought back to the present. That is the most basic form of control we have over our mind. With a deep belly breath, we can always bring our mind back to the present, where its power is most effective.

The present is where we feel our emotions, so if there is a difficult emotion happening, we need the power of our mind there to help us deal with it. When we remain alert to where our mind's power is going, we can direct that power for the benefit of all beings.

Our mind's power is like a giant elephant. Our breath is the leash that can keep the elephant from trampling villages, making them uninhabitable. All we have to do is tug on that leash regularly and we will see our mind's power create a brilliant world.

Time Travel

The idea of time travel is amusing because we like to go to new and interesting places. It is fascinating because we are constantly trying to get away from the present moment. Wouldn't it be amazing to see what life was like when the dinosaurs walked the Earth, before any of us existed? Wouldn't it be amazing to see what the world will be like in a thousand years, after all of us are gone? Isn't it amazing that we are here, now, and able to exist?

We are traveling through time. There was a time, long ago, when we were babies. Just before that we didn't exist at all. There will be a time, in the distant future, when we will take our last breath and then stop existing. While we exist, all we do is time travel.

Because we live in the future of an ancient past, we live with the consequences of our ancestors' actions. Because we live in the ancient past of a distant future, our actions will have an impact on people in the years ahead. What you do today will set the stage for what you are able to do tomorrow. What you did yesterday, made you who you are today.

Time travel is not a fantasy. It is life. If you want to observe an amazing time, look. This is the only time this time will ever be here. If you use this moment to exercise compassion and act with kindness, the people thousands of years from now will be grateful. You will be grateful tomorrow.

One Step

If you are not happy, you are only ever one step away from happiness. It can seem like a huge step, but it is a tiny step. In space, it is no step at all. You can sit in one spot and be miserable one moment, then return to happiness the next. Your fundamental condition is happiness. When you start to think about things, you obscure that happiness. No matter how far away you think you may be, you are always just that one step away.

It is not necessarily easy to take the step back to your basic happiness. It can be extremely difficult to see just how and where to step. It can be hard to move your foot. You may take a thousand steps before you take that one monumental step.

Taking the step is wonderful, but knowing that happiness is so close can be liberating. If you worry that your happiness is blocked by complex neuroses, rooted in an early childhood experience, or something you cannot change, then you may think that you need to navigate a convoluted maze to reconnect with your happiness. When you know that at any time you can take that single, simple step, the maze becomes manageable.

To take the step, you have to believe that the step is available to you right now. When you know it is there, you don't need to take it. You are free to live with your complex neuroses and travel your maze. When you sense your fundamental happiness, you don't need to grasp it. You can walk your path with confidence that every step is the one.

The Middle Path

When we walk the middle path, we pay attention to our tendencies to seek pleasure and avoid pain. Although the aim of Buddhism is to save all sentient beings from suffering, that is different from avoiding pain. In order to transcend suffering, we have to accept our pain and our pleasure.

Life happens in the present moment. Sometimes the present is painful and sometimes it is pleasurable. Pleasure taken too far will become pain, as excessive drinking can lead to a hangover. Painful experiences also contain subtle or overt pleasures, like the peace discovered in the midst of a good cry.

Walking the middle path is certainly not seeking pain and avoiding pleasure. It is appreciating where you are, when you are there. If you are excitedly looking forward to a birthday party, you are feeling the pleasure of anticipation and the pain of impatience. Reaching for the pleasure is causing some pain, but no great suffering.

When you accept pain and pleasure as they occur, you are allowed to be sad when you are sad and happy when you are happy. You always know that beneath these external circumstances, your Original Nature is shining brightly.

Where You Are

Where you are in life is where you need to be. You need to be where you are, because that is where you are. You breathe air because you need to breathe air. When you are a child, you need to be a child. When you are a teenager, you need to be a teenager. When you are an adult, you need to be an adult. As you move through these periods of your life, your understanding of life changes. Your ability to cope changes. Because everything is always changing, it is helpful to develop an appreciation for where you are.

Young children can dance unselfconsciously because they hear music. When they get cranky, they scream and cry and look to their parents for comfort. Older children forget how to dance freely and learn when and where to scream and cry. They find delight in being with other children. Teenagers know how important friends are, but they can forget how to find comfort in their parents. Adults can forget how important friends are and even forget how to scream and cry. They learn to comfort their parents and their children. With all the major changes that life brings, it's easy to feel lost and think that you should be somewhere where you are not. That is the perfect time to try to appreciate where you are.

You are where you need to be and you are moving. Soon you will be somewhere else. You will learn some new ways of thinking and you will forget some old ways. As much as you need to learn new ways, you need to forget old ways. You need to do this because that is what will happen anyway. You can scream, cry or dance right from where you are to where you need to be.

Cosmic Accounting

There are certain absolutes in life. You either get it or you don't. You are pregnant or not. You are alive or dead. You are suffering or not suffering. These are all conditions that come and go. One minute you're pregnant, the next, you are a mother. Sometimes you get it, sometimes you don't. You are alive right up until you are dead. You suffer, then you stop suffering. This is how you pass time.

You can think of time as a series of moments where things appear and disappear. You are the accountant who keeps tabs of what is and isn't in each of these moments. Your suffering comes from your attachment to the bottom line. As you count what is and isn't, you want some things to keep being, other things not to be at all, and you wish for new things to come into being. You participate by maintaining, destroying and creating things as you keep your running tally. The bottom line is quite complicated and somewhat arbitrary, also changing with you and passing time.

As complicated as it is to keep track of the accounting as it relates to your experience, if you add your family into the mix, what is and isn't becomes vague. You may not be pregnant, but your sister is. Your sister may be enjoying the moment, but your brother is suffering. Your mother may be alive, but your grandmother is dead. Your family is then alive and dead, suffering and content, pregnant and not.

Also, you can think of time as a single span in which you are born, live and die. In an eternal moment, you are alive and dead, suffering and enjoying, getting it and forgetting it. As an accountant, there is nothing to figure or become attached to anymore. Everything cancels itself out.

To create a bottom line that can tell you whether or not to suffer, you have to limit your focus to yourself in a particular moment. In that moment you can see what is, was and could be and decide if you like it or not. Then it changes.

Zen Hope

When the world seems hopeless, Zen offers a simple cure for hopelessness. To get rid of hopelessness, all you need is hope. Hollow hope is not enough. If you stay up all night hoping that the sun won't come up, you'll be sorely disappointed in the morning. The hope that Zen provides is more like hoping that the sun will come up.

To find hope in Zen you don't have to look any further than your self. You can look directly at your hopelessness. When you think that you are incapable of experiencing happiness, the hope that Zen provides is the assurance that you are wrong. Although we generally prefer to be right, it can be liberating to recognize that we are wrong. When you look at your hopelessness and see that you are wrong, a crack will appear in your wall. When you look at your self and see that you are capable and deserving of happiness, you immediately find a bit of happiness. The sun comes up.

When you're feeling hopeless, you get lots of wrong ideas about your self. Zen has a long history of wisdom and simplicity that has helped millions of people look directly at themselves, destroy those wrong ideas, and find happiness.

The world goes around. The Sun only goes down from your point of reference on the surface of the Earth. Happiness is always available to you. I hope you can see that.

Everything Zen

Zen philosophy tells us that the universe is contained in each grain of sand. The universe is amazing. It is full of everything we know and everything we don't know. It has planets, stars, galaxies, black holes, matter, antimatter, life, consciousness, and sand. A grain of sand is not so amazing. If we go to a beach, we may appreciate the sand, but in our daily lives we generally sweep it out of our homes with the all the thrill of doing chores. It is simply another grain of sand that happens to contain the entire universe.

If the entire universe is in a grain of sand, then it is also in you and me, and chimpanzees, and cement trucks and French Impressionism. To see everything connected to everything else is a Zen way of seeing the world. It may seem like an amazing way of looking at things or it may seem a silly way of looking at things. It is both. It recognizes both the majesty and ordinariness of creation. When you look at the world through a Zen lens, you see that everything is Zen.

When everything is Zen, Zen loses all meaning. Zen ideas are just ideas. Zen practice is just sitting. Zen entices people into practice with wonderfully exotic rituals, which wrap the fundamental boredom of the universe in fancy paper. The wrapping makes people interested enough in the boredom to see that it contains an incredible universe. Zen is nothing, that, and everything. It's simply amazing.

A Way We Go

In looking for the way, we each go our way. We imagine an ideal way. We see pictures of people, in love, on mountaintops, or beaches and believe they have found the way. We read about writers sitting in cafes and believe they have found the way. We imagine people dancing freely around fires and under the stars, not thinking about yesterday or tomorrow. Everywhere we turn, we encounter images of people and places that inspire peace, confidence and awe in us. They seem to have found the way through existence. Compared to those beautiful, inspiring, static images, our own way of doing things and experiencing the world can seem dull or depressing.

The way we go is not inherently dull and depressing. It is dynamic. It is constantly changing. There is no happily ever after, because ever after keeps unfolding with each moment. That is our way. The way we have come is behind us. Ahead of us is an incomprehensible world of possibilities. In each moment, all we can do is choose a way. Then, away we go.

Not Feeling It?

The self-help ideas of new age thinking, Buddhism, Taoism, mindfulness and such are fairly simple in theory. The simple prescription for happiness is to live in the here and now, pay attention to your thoughts, and be nice to yourself and others. What happens if you know all of that, but still struggle with happiness? What happens is you feel frustrated and miserable. It's not so easy just to live in the here and now, watching your thoughts and being nice to people.

Living in the here and now is difficult when the here and now feels miserable. When you feel miserable, it is obvious just how difficult it is to escape the here and now. The present seems more like a trap than a gateway to freedom. Watching your thoughts is no help, because your thoughts just confirm how difficult the here and now can be and how reasonable it is to be miserable. All that's left is being nice to yourself and others. That is good place to start.

Being nice to yourself and others prevents your problem thoughts from seeping into your behavior and making things worse. When you see what you are thinking while you try to be nice, you notice all the thoughts you entertain that aren't nice. When you hold an ideal of living in the here and now, you also notice when your thoughts are drifting into the past and future. You can see how those thoughts interact with your moods. As you pay close attention to your thoughts and moods and time and kindness, you may notice little slivers of the here and now that seem more tolerable.

The simple ideal of living in the here and now, watching your thoughts and being nice to yourself and others, is a helpful practice for getting you through a difficult here and now. It's not really such a good prescription for happiness. It is a good prescription for misery. That's when you need it. When you feel happy, your thoughts are amusing, the here and now is joyful and it's still a good idea practice being nice to yourself and others.

Appearing and Disappearing

Everything changes. Things are always appearing and disappearing. Moment to moment, hour to hour, year to year, things come and go. We look at things like mountains and the moon and think nothing changes. We feel our moods and think that they are like mountains. Moods change much more noticeably than mountains. Thoughts change even faster than moods. Thoughts appear and disappear. Moods appear and disappear. We appear and disappear. The entire universe as it existed one second ago, is entirely different now. Watching things appear and disappear and allowing them to do that can make room for understanding to appear…and disappear.

Clean Slate

Being able to start over is an amazing gift. Every moment gives us the opportunity to wipe our slate clean and start again. In each moment of our lives, we recreate ourselves. We have developed a pattern for what we think we are, so we replicate ourselves as faithfully as possible each time. Even when we are not happy with who we are, we make ourselves that way again and again. Even when we know exactly what and how we want to change, we recreate ourselves complete with obstacles to that change.

Each moment is a clean slate. We create ourselves with our actions. We create our actions with our thoughts. Our thoughts pour into us from a great abyss which is a Clean Slate. Our thoughts pour into our heads and rattle around creating emotions. Our emotions will tell us how we are doing. We will feel good, bad, or neutral. If we cycle through these feelings quickly, good, neutral, bad, neutral, good, bad, neutral, we can see how the feelings relate to the thoughts. If we get stuck in a rut, we will feel bad, neutral, bad, neutral, bad and it won't seem to matter what we think, we feel the same way. That is when it is time to go back to a clean slate. Throw out your beliefs, wipe your slate clean and watch your thoughts pour in from the Source.

Time and Space

As you watch your thoughts pour in from the Clean Slate to your clean slate, only act on the thoughts that lead to good feelings and recreate yourself with kindness and compassion. If you find yourself in a rut again, do it again. You can do this a thousand times a day. As you get better, then you can do it a hundred times a day, then just a few times a day. When you get really good, you'll see that you are just a clean slate and you won't worry at all about reinventing yourself. You will continue to recreate yourself and each new manifestation of you will be filled with happiness.

When Will Life Get Easier?

Life can get easier at any time, or it can get harder. When we are really young, we don't even know that life can be hard. As soon as life starts to feel hard, we imagine that it will get easier when we get older. When we're a little older, we can remember that life wasn't always so easy, but we know that it was a little easier, before we worried about who liked us and who we liked. At that age, we still think that things will get easier when we get older. When we get older, we start to look back fondly on our vague memories of when we were in school and things were easier. We look forward to retirement, when we can relax and enjoy our golden years. When we get to that age, things hurt. We worry about our children and grandchildren and have a cautious eye on death. At that point, we know that life was easy at times and difficult at times, but we imagine that it was easier back when. For life to become easier, you have to know that it can. You have to find some peace with life, death and your sense of self.

If you imagine that you can achieve a circumstance in your life that will make it easier, you can work toward that circumstance. You may be disappointed when you achieve the circumstance and life remains difficult. You can get all kinds of fame and fortune, and in doing so, create all kinds of complicated problems for yourself.

If you want life to be easy, you need to simplify your life. Forget about yourself. Know that you are capable, unique, and wonderful, then forget about yourself. When you stop worrying about you, you are free to see things as they are. If you like somebody, you take pleasure in their company. If something makes you sad, you cry. If you make a mistake, apologize. If you are curious, ask questions. When you recognize how difficult situations and emotions come and go and that you survive intact, you stop worrying about yourself. Whenever that happens, life gets easier now.

Chapter 4

Meditation and Mindfulness

The Purpose of Meditation

The purpose of meditation is to improve your life. When your life is well and fully improved, then you can think about the purposelessness of meditation. Meditation becomes purposeless when you notice that your life cannot be improved, not because it is hopeless, but because it is perfect. Imagining that your life is perfect is not quite the same as noticing it. If you feel like your life could and should be improved and you console yourself with the idea that you are likely perfect despite the evidence, then you will continue to gather evidence to shoot holes in your perfect theory. If you happen to be doing dishes or raking the yard and it hits you that everything is absolutely as it is, as it has been and as it will be, and you are somehow okay with that, then you will not give another thought to improving your life. Until that time, it is reasonable to meditate with a purpose.

In real life it is impossible to mediate without a purpose. Nobody accidentally finds themselves in a zendo staring at a wall, enduring leg cramps and brain farts. That is done on purpose. People don't miraculously get up an hour early every day and set aside 20 minutes every evening to sit quietly and count their breaths. That is a purposeful discipline. Once you are sitting, purpose begins to dissolve. You can't will yourself to see the Light. You can only see what you will, hear what you do and think what you may. On many occasions you may think that meditation is a waste of time or purposeless. On many other occasions you may think that your life has improved.

Applied Zen

Zen is both a way of life and a philosophy. When people get absorbed in a beautiful scene or find serenity in the midst of a hectic life, they may describe the experience as zen. People talk about living in the moment as zen. If you are able to appear calm and rational when all hell is breaking loose around you, you may be described as zen. These are a few examples of how zen has crept into our language and our way of thinking. If you don't practice Zen Buddhism, there are lots of ideas that come out of Zen that can help to bring you peace and happiness.

The idea that we are not separate from the universe is a helpful idea. People struggle with self-esteem and they feel all kinds of angst and sadness because they think that what they are is damaged, flawed or just not good enough. Imagining that you are continuous with the universe and that the moon is as much a part of you as your foot, can help you see beauty and splendor in yourself that you might otherwise miss.

The idea that happiness is available to you, no matter what your situation, is a good Zen idea. It's kind of like looking for the ketchup in the refrigerator. If you think that you may be out of ketchup you will stop looking and never look behind the milk. If you know that you have ketchup, you will keep looking until you find it.

Meditation and Mindfulness

The idea that a root of suffering is desire can help anybody learn to live with their wants. People confuse suffering with not having rather than wanting. When you realize that you can satisfy a desire by not wanting something, it gives you an option in trying to live with cravings.

If you don't practice Zen, Zen ideas can enrich your life. If you want to practice Zen, meditate. See for yourself just what it is that you are.

Tips for Zen Practice

The simplest advice I could suggest for somebody beginning a Zen and/or Buddhist practice is to meditate everyday for 10-30 minutes. If meditation is easy for you, do it in the morning and evening for 20-30 minutes each time. If you can meditate regularly, you can do anything.

After meditation, the next thing is to approach life as though the absolute, most important thing is getting to understand your True Nature. Your True Nature is that bit of you that is the whole universe. You are able to experience that directly when you are not thinking. When you believe that the most important thing is understanding this, then all the other important things that you think about, which cause your distress, fall away.

Meditation is a focused time to build your mindfulness muscles. The rest of your time you use your enhanced mindfulness powers to pay attention to every thought and feeling that you have. When you see that your thoughts and feelings are just thoughts and feelings, you will stop sorting them into good feelings and bad feelings. They are just thoughts, which are part of your True Nature, which is the most important thing there is. It is also wonderful.

Low Motivation

If you are suffering from low motivation, or if you are not motivated because you are suffering, there is hope for you in your hopelessness. You can do something for yourself by doing nothing. You can fill your life with emptiness. You can meditate. There's nothing to it.

Meditation can be frustrating if you use it to pry yourself out of a mood. If you meditate to achieve enlightenment, it can be a long, painful slog. Sitting there hoping, striving, and seeking a different state of mind will leave you longing to be where you are not. It takes a lot of motivation to embark on such a journey.

If you have trouble finding motivation, just sit. Waste ten minutes of your life. Think about nothing at all. Put all of your attention on your breath. Breathe in until you are full. Breathe out until you are empty. If you're still not motivated to do anything, do it again.

You can waste as much time as you have meditating. If you meditate every day, you may find yourself gaining motivation. You can then use that motivation to continue your sitting practice.

Getting Annoyed

The goal of meditation is to relieve the world of suffering. The relief usually begins with your own suffering and then it spreads to others. When you find and create peace and harmony in your life, it naturally helps others. When you don't have peace and harmony in your life, others are also affected by your condition. When you are at peace, things don't annoy you. When you are annoyed it's helpful to take note of your condition, because you are beginning to suffer.

When you meditate, you observe your thoughts. You have a point of focus, which may be your breath or a koan, and you notice as your thoughts move by that point of focus. It's like looking out of the window of a train as it starts to move. The objects in the window start to move, but the inside of the train remains still. You see the things in the window going by and you know you are moving, you are not concerned with the things outside of the window, they just remind you that you are moving. Often in meditation, thoughts carry you away from your point of focus. You start making lists, or doing math, or having conversations with people who are not there. When you remember that you're trying to focus, you come back to center.

Sitting meditation is a small part of a meditation practice. If you sit for half an hour, two times a day, you have a significant practice. That still leaves 23 hours a day to work with your mind in a less controlled environment. To carry your focus from meditation into the rest of your life, you can use your annoyances to help you. When you are not annoyed, you are centered and absorbed with the general goodness of life. When something annoys you, you forget about that peaceful state of mind. That annoying something could be a thought, a friend, a family member, a stranger, or a pebble in your shoe. The thing that actually annoys you is always the thought about the annoying situation.

  Like when you meditate, when you notice that you are annoyed, you remember who you are, see what you are thinking, let the thought go and refocus. Like your breath, annoyances are always there. You can use them in your practice to relieve suffering and bring peace to the world.

Getting Angry

No matter how zen you may be, you will also get angry. Anger is a difficult emotion. It does not always feel as awful as sadness, but it can more destructive. Anger has a dangerous aspect of demanding immediate action. It can be easier to sit with other emotions and wait for them to pass. With anger, you feel compelled to do something about it. It is important to recognize when you are angry, so that your angry actions do not cause unnecessary suffering for yourself or those around you.

Your anger always causes suffering in you. It is generally a combination of hurt and sadness that brings about anger. That is two kinds of suffering rolled into one. Acting in anger is how we try to relieve our suffering. Often, in attempting to alleviate our suffering, we inflict it on others. When we are angry, we may feel that the others deserve to experience the suffering we choose to inflict. That is not true. Nobody should suffer.

When you are angry, it may be difficult to remember that and especially difficult to imagine that it could be true. That is why it is important to reserve a special form of mindfulness for when you are angry. You can use that mindfulness to help reduce your suffering and avoid passing it on to others.

Getting angry produces a lot of energy. Sometimes that energy feels good. When you are mindful, you are aware of the good and bad feelings of anger. It is important to notice both so that you don't fall into the trap of getting angry as a means of accessing that good feeling. More suffering than good comes out of anger and the person that suffers most consistently is the angry person.

Like any suffering, anger is a good teacher. It comes and goes. It can carry you away and it can burn down your kingdom. If you pay close attention to your anger, you can prevent the fires from burning. With enough focused attention you can find peace from your anger. When you learn to master anger, then you can start working on desire. Desire can drive you mad.

Meditate

To get the most out of meditation, don't try to get anything out of meditation. Just sit. Sit once or twice a day and make a habit of it. Meditating every day for a little time will serve you better than meditating every now and again for a long time.

When you meditate, sit in a quiet place where you won't be interrupted. Set a timer to keep track of your session. Most smart phones have timers on them. If you get sleepy when you meditate, try it first thing in the morning and keep your back straight. If you have trouble falling asleep at night, try it before you go to bed.

Meditating is not thinking, it is just sitting. Sit and pay attention to your breathing. Breathe from your belly, in your nose and out of your mouth. When you notice yourself thinking about anything, focus on your breath.

While you meditate, don't try to get anything out of meditation. Don't worry if you are doing well or poorly. If you are sitting, you are doing well. The only time that you try to get something out of meditation is when you decide to develop the habit. At that point, you commit to changing your life. Then you just sit. Your life will change itself.

Finding Balance

If you are looking for balance in your life, stand up straight and breathe deeply. You will find that you are perfectly balanced. Your life may seem more complicated. You may be looking for balance between home and work, proteins and fats, alone time and social time, worry and wonder, serotonin and cortisol, or happiness and sadness. In many of these areas you have balance, in others you may need to create balance.

Creating balance requires changing your behavior and habits. If you begin your day by standing straight and taking a deep breath, you begin your day with balance. If you sit straight for 15-20 minutes and watch your breath, you will see where in your life that you need to create balance. You shouldn't think about where you need to create balance, you should just focus on your breath. If you do this every day, maybe twice a day, other parts of your life will find their balance.

If you are walking on a tight rope, all your focus is on the rope. There is no room for other thoughts. The rope will hold you up. In you life, your breath is your rope. In anything that you do, you can focus on your breath and you will find balance.

Steppingstones

Practicing meditation is like placing steppingstones in our stream of thought. In our mind, the water is always flowing. Sometimes it is a creek, a trickle through a rocky bed, which is easy to traverse. Sometimes it is a rushing stream that presents more challenges. Other times it is a river that seems intimidating or impossible to cross without drowning. Having a readily available supply of steppingstones can bring us great comfort on our journey. It can save our life.

When we sit in meditation, the water continues to flow, and we observe its passing. We can see our thoughts without them carrying us away. We have a solid refuge in our daily routine that allows us to pass through life's currents without getting our toes wet.

When we place steppingstones regularly through our life, even the most turbulent river becomes manageable. With consistent practice, the steppingstones become a bridge. After that, we just walk on water.

Stories, Feelings, and Compassion

Every feeling comes with a story. The story is the reason behind the feeling. That reason could be big or small. You may feel bad, because you haven't achieved what you hoped for in life, or you may feel angry because somebody criticized your work. In both cases you are feeling bad. The reason that you feel bad is the story.

When you focus on the story, you can go on and on in your mind with *whys* and *hows* and *what ifs*. There is no end to stories. To focus on the feeling, breathe deeply, feel where the feeling is in your body. Feel whether it's in your chest or stomach or head. Explore it with a sense of curiosity, as though you don't know anything about it. Continue to breathe consciously, with your attention focused on the feeling, and you may notice that the it is tolerable. You will find that feelings are manageable, even when they are uncomfortable.

Focusing your attention on feelings as they happen, gives you a sense of control. You can't make the feelings go away, but you can observe the source of your discomfort. As you observe the feelings, they change. Observing is the closest you can come to controlling them. Like children behave differently if they know an adult is watching them, your thoughts and feelings respond to your attention.

Hear Now

To transform negative feelings, fill your attention with compassion. Be kind to yourself in your thoughts as you explore your feelings. It's too bad that you are feeling these difficult emotions. You deserve understanding and peace.

Ugly Shoes

The problem with accepting things as they are is that we don't always like how things are. When things seem terrible why would we accept them? If you buy a pair of shoes, take them home and decide that you don't like them, you don't accept them as they are, you return them. This ability we have to return anything we don't like can get in the way of accepting things as they are.

We like to think of ourselves as powerful. We like to be active in the world, bringing about justice and the changes that we want. The idea of accepting things as they are seems passive and weak when we don't like how things are. If we are feeling miserable, accepting things as they are feels like giving up all power and resigning ourselves to our misery. Yet, our misery is caused by not accepting things as they are.

Accepting things as they are is the first step in changing things. If you bring home a pair of shoes that you don't like. First you accept that you brought home a pair of ugly shoes, then you return them. Accepting things as they are has nothing to do with liking or not liking. Acceptance is just recognizing how things are. What you do with how things are is up to you.

Moody Weather

Moods come and go. If you think of moods like the weather, they are beyond your control and you take what you get. If you think of moods like a mirror, then your actions influence what happens in the reflection. If you just feel your moods, they will seem like the weather. If you pay attention to your moods, you may see yourself moving the image in the mirror.

To pay attention to your mood, start by feeling your mood. Notice what mood you are feeling and hold it in your awareness. As you pay attention to your mood, notice physical sensations associated with it. Notice the thoughts that sustain your mood. Notice external sensations, like the sun, the wind, dogs barking, birds singing or music playing. Notice your breathing. As you notice these other sensations, keep your awareness on your mood. Soon, you will notice your mood change. When you practice paying attention to your moods you become familiar with their comings and goings. Each bad mood doesn't feel so ominous and each good mood is still enjoyable.

If you don't pay attention to your mood, you just feel your mood. You go about your life and moods happen to you. You feel either good, bad, or neither. Your mood becomes like the weather. If it's rainy, it's rainy and you get wet. If it's sunny, it's sunny and you dry off. Like the weather, you don't seem to have any control over the moods. Although you don't have any control over your moods, they respond to your circumstance. So, in order to influence your mood, you constantly try to address your circumstances. If you're sad because you're lonely, you run around trying to find company. When you just feel your moods, without paying attention to them, they can seem overwhelming. Like a hurricane, a bad mood can be devastating.

Although paying attention to moods does not give you total control over your moods, it provides perspective. As soon as you start to pay attention, you become grounded in the present. By locating yourself in the present moment you can notice your thoughts. If you notice your thoughts making wild claims that you would never believe in a different mood, you can correct those thoughts. By breathing and connecting with your senses, you can slow your thoughts down a little, or take a break from them. Checking in with the present can prevent a mood from getting away from you. Instead of a hurricane, you get a shower. As you pay attention to the shower, you can watch the clouds part and feel the Sun again. When you practice paying attention to your moods, you will get used to seeing the sun come out and you won't mind the rain so much.

Mood Matters

Moods matter. The difference between being happy and being sad is your mood. The rest is all the same. Moods matter because they impact how you interact with the world. If you don't pay attention to your moods, your moods will seem like a reflection of how things are. You will forget how things really are.

If you think things are how you feel about them, your interactions will create problems for you. If you see a cute and cuddly grizzly bear, and you feel so wonderful that you go tickle its belly, there could be problems. If you pay attention to your mood, you can observe your happiness and the grizzly bear from a comfortable distance.

It matters immensely if you are happy, sad, scared or angry. You should know what you are at all times. You do not need to congratulate yourself for being happy or berate yourself for being angry, but know what you are and know that you are much more than that.

Anxiety Awareness

When you learn mindfulness, you learn to focus on your breathing and to observe your thoughts so that you can find peace in the present moment. Breathing is the great tool of mindfulness because it is always there and it has a physiological connection with relaxation. It is beautiful and peaceful. When you are not thinking about your breathing it is still there for you, just like your essential goodness.

Anxiety is another great tool of mindfulness. It is not always there, but it is always waiting in the wings. Your life is cruising along and you're feeling peaceful, then, suddenly, anxiety springs itself on you and breaks you out of your pleasant mood.

There is nothing pleasant or welcome about anxiety. If you liked it, it wouldn't be anxiety. Feeling anxious can bring you into the present moment as effectively as breathing. When you notice yourself feeling anxious, you are present. You are whole. You are all that you can be, and you are anxious.

When you engage with your anxiety by meeting it with your breath and observing your thoughts, you gain a sense of control. Each time you encounter your anxiety with your breath, you can see what happens to it and to you rather than being carried away by it. You will learn to break its spell.

When your anxiety can no longer bewitch you, it will go away.

If you consistently practice meeting your anxiety with mindfulness, over time, your anxiety will come less, leave sooner, and won't be so painful. You won't worry about its comings and goings because when it comes you know how to breathe into it, let it go, and return to your peace.

Controlling Emotions

To control your emotions, give up the idea of control. Emotions are part of your being. They happen all the time. If you were able to control your emotions, you would be able to stop them. You would be able to choose which emotions to have when. If that were the case, you would always choose to be happy and you would have no problems. If you want to choose to be happy, you have to be able to handle the unchosen emotions like sadness, fear, or anxiety. It is worth trying to control these emotions, because when they are out of control, they conspire to ruin your life.

Controlling emotions is difficult because it's hard to tell what is an emotion and what is supposed to be controlling it. When you experience fear, it takes you over. What is supposed to control the fear is consumed by it. You can't just make it stop, because you are afraid. You are fear. When you notice that you are fear, then you are no longer fear. You are something separate, safer, and you have some control.

By paying close attention to your emotional highs and lows, you learn to see the play of emotion. The emotion is separate from you and it is separate from the thought, or story, that justifies it. If you are sad because your goldfish died, then you can experience sadness. The sadness is something different from you and it is something different from your goldfish dying. Eventually you will be happy and your goldfish will still be dead. That is only the current story attached to your sadness. Your sadness has been there before with other stories and it will come again with new stories.

    When you pay attention to your emotions, self, thoughts, and stories, you come as close as you can to controlling emotions. Although you can't pick when to feel what, you can put each emotion in its context, knowing that you are capable of surviving any and all emotions available to humankind. When you learn to observe and find comfort in the difficult emotions, the more pleasant emotion of joy will spring forth much more freely, as if you had chosen it.

Letting Go

We all know that in order to find peace and happiness we just have to let go. Like all simple advice, letting go is not easy. One of the reasons that it is so difficult to let go is that we have to let go of something. We have to let go of our egos or we have to let go of our neuroses. We have to let our habits go. We have to let our desires and our anger go. It can be difficult or impossible to let these things go. Another thing we need to do is let go of is how we think about letting go.

To find peace and happiness, we don't have to actively release things, that is not letting go, that is allowing to leave. Letting go is even more passive. Let things go as they go. Things go as they go and we have to find peace in that.

If there is a freight train barreling along the tracks, let it pass. If you decide not to let it pass and stand on the tracks in front of it, it passes anyway. You get obliterated.

Letting go is like being a mirror. A mirror reflects everything without passing judgment or grabbing onto the images that appear on its surface. It lets things come and go.

Although we are mirrors reflecting things as they go, we are also a participants interacting with things. Letting things go does not mean that we don't interact with the world. Our actions, reactions and interactions are part of all that we are letting go.

Our anger, desire and ego tricks come and go and we are aware of it all. If we resist, it happens. If we let it happen, it happens as it happens. It's happening. Let it go.

Good and Bad

Dividing the world into good and bad is one of our favorite pastimes. It is also a source of our confusion. Because the sorting is an unconscious habit, we don't decide, we just know. When we smell something bad, it is bad. When we taste something good, it is good. The good thing about dividing everything into good and bad is that we learn to appreciate what is good. The bad part is that we can't stop.

We confuse ourselves by always playing good and bad, because we think good is actually good and bad is actually bad. We believe that we have good and bad days. We think we have good and bad feelings. We think we are good and bad people. We can't quit.

If we quit playing this sorting game, we could see things more clearly. We would notice when our pleasure turns into pain, and we could let our pain go when it passes. We wouldn't feel bad for not feeling good. We wouldn't feel bad for feeling sad, or mad, or lonely. We would just feel sad, or mad, or lonely. When we stop dividing things into good and bad, we don't end up with neutral, we discover life's fundamental goodness. Not bad.

A Positive Light

If you try to look at your troubles in a positive light, you may miss your troubles. They do not come in a positive light, that's why they are troubles. Trying to see your troubles in a positive light, it's like going to the movies and trying to watch a play. That's not what's playing at the movies.

Some obstacles are challenges and some are problems. If you do a crossword puzzle, you are taking on a world of problems for fun. It is a challenge, not a problem. A crossword puzzle comes in a positive light. It looks like fun. A toothache comes in a painful light. It hurts.

There is a positive light beneath everything. It will shine through when the time comes. When you see the positive light, you are not pretending, you are just seeing it. Knowing that the positive light is beneath it all, gives you the courage to look at the rest of the world in whatever light it has.

If life gives you lemons, taste the sourness, that's what makes lemonade so delicious. If you are not bursting with happiness, feel what you are feeling. You will see that you are capable of handling the whole spectrum of emotions. You will see that you can handle any situation. You can handle your troubles. Your troubles will teach you just what you need to know. You don't need to love them, but if you look at them, closely, bravely, they will start to break apart. The light will shine through the cracks.

Finding Your Happiness

Becoming happy is not a simple matter. If you could find happiness by copying somebody else's behavior, everybody would only have to act like the happy guy. It would be nice and simple. If you could find happiness by creating some new habits and dropping some old habits, that would take a little work, but it would be worth it. If there were somebody out there who could read your mind and flip a switch to make you happy, people would be lining up to offer up their minds. Happiness is one of the most important thing you can achieve in life, but it is not a realistic goal in itself. Your happiness is a byproduct of thinking and acting in a certain way that is completely unique to you.

Finding your happiness is like finding the Sun. You know that the Sun is there whether you can see it or not. All day you see its light. All night you have confidence the light will be back the next day. Knowing that your happiness is there, you can forget about it and pay attention to what you think and do. When you know happiness is around, you are free to notice just how you feel other than happy. You can give each feeling its time without resentment.

To find your happiness, it helps to think about happiness, sadness, anger, and fear for yourself and others. Happiness is there. When you don't worry about finding it, it will find you.

Happiness Happens

Knowing that you are not your moods and that your moods will pass is like base camp when you're climbing a mountain. You still need to climb. There are lots of things you can do to help improve your mood.

I always advocate for mindfulness and meditation. Mindfulness is paying attention to your thoughts, so that you don't accidentally cut yourself down by thinking horrible or negative things about yourself as you pass through low moods. Meditation is sitting still and actively watching your thoughts for ten or twenty minutes once or twice a day. If sitting still is too difficult then yoga, exercise, or going for walks can help to lift your spirits. Look for beauty everywhere. Notice small feelings of happiness. Spend time with people who make you feel good. Although your moods will pass, you can do things to help them pass more quickly.

Happiness is not your goal, life is the goal, happiness will happen.

No Complaints

If you want to have no complaints, stop complaining. Complaining is a symptom of the basic dissatisfaction of life. It is the natural response to suffering. It is habit forming. One of the obstacles to becoming happy is the social encouragement of complaining. Even if you are feeling pretty well, there is always something not quite right that you can use to spark a conversation. If you fall into the habit of exchanging complaints with your friends and family, then you may start to believe that all of life's little annoyances are actually bad. You will be ever vigilant for problems so that you have something to talk about.

Mindfulness can help you combat a complaining habit. If you spend a day noticing all of your complaints, you will see just how ingrained the habit is in your outlook. If you notice just the complaints that find their way into your speech, you will see who your complaining buddies are. If you notice all the complaints that cross your mind, you will see how you resist life.

When you remain mindful of complaints, your unconscious complaining will stop. You will be slightly amused by your reaction to perceived problems. You will also notice how people around you complain, but you won't get sucked into the idea that the world is a series of minor and major inconveniences. You will build some immunity to negativity. Of course you can, and will, still complain, just for fun, but you will know that beneath it all, life is good.

Common Sense

Whatever it is that's happening, we are constantly trying to make sense of it. There is so much going on though, that we cannot make sense of it. We try anyway. We develop an understanding that passes for sense. We compare our sense of things with other people's sense of things and together we come up with common sense. Some aspects of our common sense are sensible; others are absurd. When we try to live our lives dutifully, following the absurd aspects of common sense, we start to suffer.

We are told that if we work hard and stay in school, we will get a nice job and make plenty of money and be happy. We may do all these things, then notice that we are no happier than a person who made a Youtube video and got a gazillion views. Then common sense would tell us that fame and acknowledgement should make us happy. Then we notice that the Youtube phenom is in rehab.

Sometimes following common sense leads us to happiness, sometimes it leads us to rehab. Sometimes rehab leads us to happiness. The only common sense that can reliably lead us to happiness is our sense of taste, touch, smell, sight, sound and thought. Any two people can smell a rose and, although it will be a different experience for each of them, they will certainly experience a common scent. They will feel connected to each other and to the rose, and there will be a sense of peace in the experience.

When trying to live by society's sense of common sense leads you into a place of suffering, you can recognize that you have been lead astray, into an abyss of absurdity, and bring yourself back to reality by observing your immediate surroundings through your senses. It can be a delightful bit of rehab. It's quite sensible.

Kissing Boo-Boos

Mindfulness is like kissing boo-boos. When a child skins their knee or stubs their toe and their parent kisses the place that hurts, the child feels better. Kissing boo boos works. Mindfulness works the same way.

When a child experiences a minor bump and feels pain, the pain consumes them. Their reaction is to run away from the pain. They cry and run to their mommy or daddy to make everything better. By kissing the boo-boo, the parent takes the child's focus, which is scrambling to get away from the pain, and focuses it on the source of the pain. When a loving kiss is applied to the source of pain, the pain can be felt, accepted, associated with love, and the situation is under control. Balance is restored.

When you are older and suffer from emotional boo-boos, you can use mindfulness to kiss those boo-boos too. General mindfulness alerts you to your mood. With more focused mindfulness, you can watch the thoughts that contribute to your mood. When you notice yourself thinking hurtful things about yourself or others, you just kiss the boo-boo. Don't judge the thought. Don't scold yourself for having the thought. Just recognize the thought as a hurtful thought and kiss it away with loving kindness. With each mindful kiss, a boo-boo gets better. Keep kissing those boo boos and you will feel a sense of control. Balance will be restored.

Chapter 5

Love and Enlightenment

Being Enlightened

Imagine enlightenment as a profound sense of inner peace, a connectedness to all living things and immense compassion for other people's suffering. This experience would change your outlook on life. It would change the way you think of yourself. It would change the way you perceive others. It would change how you interact with others. When you understand how everybody suffers, and recognize that they don't even understand why they are suffering, you naturally want to help guide them out of the darkness. You feel joy in your life.

Becoming enlightened is like winning the spiritual lottery. If winning the lottery is your goal, you have to buy a lottery ticket. If becoming enlightened is your goal, you have to be enlightened. Your odds at becoming enlightened are much better than winning the lottery. Enlightenment is your natural state. You just have to fall back into it.

Falling into enlightenment can happen at any time, or never. To become an enlightened being you shouldn't wait for that spark of realization to change your life. You should just act as though you are enlightened. When you interact with other people, be kind and compassionate. Recognize their suffering. Act as though inner peace is your natural state and take whatever comes your way as it comes. Speak the truth, because that is all that matters.

You can go about all of your regular business as an enlightened being, keeping in mind that peace and harmony are more important than most regular goals. When you notice yourself suffering, feel compassion for yourself and for everybody else who suffers too. Filled with compassion, you can offer your suffering to the world in the name of peace.

It can be a long, hard road to realizing your enlightenment. In the meantime just be enlightened.

The Path of Peace

There are a million paths to peace. Peace is everywhere. You're standing on it, sitting in it or lying under it. You may be walking through it, or running by it. It may enter you through your eyes, nose, mouth, ears, skin or mind. It can spread from you through your breath, thoughts, words and actions. If you are not at peace, then you are on a path toward peace.

There is inner peace and outer peace. Inner peace is feeling fine about how things are. Outer peace is getting along with the people around you and being in harmony with your environment. Inner peace inspires outer peace, which inspires inner peace. Noticing peace and valuing peace is the path to peace. Noticing unrest, anger, violence, needs, desires, and pain in yourself and others is also the path to peace.

If you get tired and frustrated on the path to peace, just stop, rest, look, listen, and breathe. You are there. It's not really your path. It is the path of peace and you're on it.

The Five Desires

Buddhism is fun because it teaches that everything is one, then it neatly divides that oneness into categories.

The most basic Buddhist teaching is the four noble truths that suffering happens, there is a cause, there is a cure and there is a method to the cure. The method is the eightfold path of right view, right thought, right speech, right action, right livelihood, right effort, right mindfulness, and right concentration. So if you can live by the eightfold path and do everything right, you will stop suffering. The impediments to all that correct living are the three poisons, anger, ignorance and desire. Anger is anger, ignorance is thinking that you are two instead of one, and desire has five nice, neat categories.

The five desires fly in the face of our normal way of thinking about wants and needs. If you are accustomed to the Ten Commandments, where it is clear what thou shalt and shalt not do, then you need to shift gears to think about the five desires. The five desires are desires for money, fame, food, sex and sleep (not necessarily in that order).

If you take a shalt-not approach to these desires, then you will soon become exhausted and die without sleep or food. These desires are not good or bad, they are integral parts of your life. They are points for awareness. It is not bad to have desires, but it is good to be able to recognize them. Desires are not evil, but they can be distracting.

Despite what you may think, as you learn to be aware of your desires, it is possible to become rich and famous, eat well, make love, sleep soundly and still be happy.

The Antidote

Here, drink this. With one sip, the world will open up to you anew. The problems you have been carrying will crumble. The pain you have been feeling will vanish and an intense pleasure will fill the void. Any inkling of isolation you have felt will melt away and you will feel tremendous love lifting your spirit.

This antidote is 100% natural ingredients. It may cause you to lose your ambition, but you won't have to abandon your goals. Your goals may change. You may become obsessed with distributing the antidote. You may want to help others see what you see, feel what you feel, to understand that they are as connected as you. Although this antidote is specifically for you, once you have consumed it, you will recognize that it is available to everyone.

This? This is water. Delicious. The antidote is already in you.

That's That

Everything happens for a reason. The reason is that it happens. Everything will turn out fine in the end, because everything was fine in the beginning. It is also fine in the middle. When you are in the middle of it, you are alive. In the beginning, you are not born yet. In the end, you are dead. If you are alive, then you have the opportunity to witness it all.

One of the things that makes it so amazing, is that it does not go according to plan. You have these fantastic plans, so when things go according to plan, you feel wonderful and in control. When things stray from the plan, you feel at the mercy of the elements and afraid. Either way it unfolds is just how it happens.

If something happens wildly off plan and you imagine a spiritual intelligence making things happen for that mysterious reason, you imagine that the reason is for the greater good. You have faith that good will come of every situation. If you know that the good is there, and see it right there, where you are looking, that is good.

When you expect to see good everywhere and you see bad, or feel bad, you start to doubt your faith because your faith tells you that even bad is good. If you have faith that bad is good, but still see bad, then that is bad. That is good. Good is bad. Bad is good. Good is good. Bad is bad. That is That.

Alright not All Right

So much of our worry comes from hoping nothing will go wrong, ever. Things will go wrong, but you will be alright. It certainly won't be all right. If you are prone to worry, stress and anxiety, something is wrong, but you are alright. Even when big, important things go wrong, you are alright.

Being alright, does not always feel alright. It often feels like something is wrong. Even if it feels like things are generally alright, one small thing going wrong could upset that balance and it will feel like things are all wrong all over again. It's not all wrong. It's not all right. That's alright.

All right is a ridiculous ideal. All wrong is just as preposterous. Things generally hum along mostly right. You get your food, you get your shelter, you love people and people love you. That is all right. Right? It is not perfect though. The food you eat is not always the most nourishing. Your room doesn't protect you from your feelings. The people you love don't always behave as they should. The people who love you don't always treat you as you would like. That's alright.

Life is lived between all right and all wrong. There are no right and wrong feelings, there are just feelings. If it feels like things are all wrong, you need to remind yourself that you are alright. If it feels like things are all right, good for you. You're alright then too.

Mind Tricks

Like a masterful magician, the mind likes to create illusions for our amusement. The mind is a mighty illusionist and it has a captive, gullible audience in us. We are completely under the mind's control. When the mind tells us we're tired, we go to sleep. When the mind tells us we're sad we cry. When the mind tells us we're happy, we rejoice. It is quite a show.

One of the mind's favorite tricks is to make us believe that our circumstances cause our moods. Life provides all kinds of interesting circumstances, such as birth and death, love and marriage, heaven and hell, rich and poor, and popular and scorned. We experience these circumstances all the time and we have feelings. The mind, crafty performer that it is, suggests that these circumstances cause our moods. After the illusion is set up, the mind just sits back and watches us react wildly to all the changing circumstances in our lives. If we don't like our moods, we wave our arms around in the smoke of our circumstances and never notice the mirror.

The mirror is the mind's greatest trick. The mirror is the thing that reflects all the smoke of the circumstance. It is a marvelous mirror that reflects taste, touch, light, sound, smell, and thoughts. We don't notice the mirror because we are too close to it. We think it is us. We care intensely about what happens in the mirror and to the mirror. We take in the senses, follow the thoughts and we create an image of ourselves. The mind lets us believe we are that image.

If we are not happy with what is happening in the mirror, we need to address the magician. We need to watch the mind. If we pay close and constant attention to the mind as it manipulates the mirror and blows smoke around our circumstances, we will be able to see through its tricks. With focused attention, we see that the interactions of circumstances and self do not dictate feelings. We will notice that love cannot really disappear. We will be impressed with our crazy creativity, and we will learn to enjoy the show. Poof.

Delusion

If we consider that our everyday reality is some kind of elaborate illusion, then we are free to question everything. Reality becomes a giant question mark and all we can do is behold it and wonder what the heck is going on. That is liberation in the midst of delusion.

There is reality and there is delusion. Reality is how things are beyond our perception. Delusion is our mind's best approximation of what is real. How can we possibly know what is real? It's hard to know for certain if there is a God, or gods, or nothing of the sort. It's hard to know if what we eat is good for us or not. It's hard to know if other people are being honest with us. It can be hard to know if we are being honest with ourselves. This is our reality. We piece together what is real, from light, sound, taste, touch and thinking. That is our delusion.

We pride ourselves in our ability to deal with reality. We rank ourselves in relation to each other based on who knows what about what. If we are all deluded, then who is more deluded than whom? These are the kinds of dilemmas that living a life of illusion present. It's okay not to know. It's okay to wonder what's going on. Although we may not know exactly what is happening, we can sense that it is special.

As It Is

There are two ways to see the world, As it is and as it isn't. As it is, is liberating. As it isn't, is a game we play. When we can't see the world as it is, we imagine how we would like it to be. This imagining is our hopes, dreams and fears. We imagine alternate realities all the time. Even the reality that we regularly experience is an alternate reality to the reality that everybody else experiences. Although we have imagined our particular reality, there is an underlying reality that we all share. We all have an image of what is real and if we don't like that image, we spend our lives trying to make it more like how we would like it to be. If we happen to recognize the underlying reality, we will love it.

 We have limited control over making things how we want them to be. We have slightly more control over recognizing the world as it is. To see the world as it is, we start from where we are. If we are hungry and hate how it feels to be hungry, then we suffer. If we are hungry and unconcerned with food or resolution, but focused on the physical sensation in our body, then we experience our hunger as it is. If we recognize our hunger and want to make the world a better place, then we eat.

 With any problem, the best way to find a resolution is to see the situation as it is and then act. You can continue to imagine how you would like the world to be and work toward that goal, but the better you are at recognizing and accepting the world as it is, the easier it will be for you to take appropriate action. The more you accept the world as it is, the less you'll suffer.

Suffering comes from desperately wanting the world to be how it isn't. Happiness comes from engaging with the world as it is.

Nothing Matters

When you feel like nothing matters, you're wrong. Nothing matters. We get all caught up in things and we forget how important nothing is. When things get noisy, nothing sounds better. When things get too busy, it's nice to do nothing for a little while. When everything is perfect, you want nothing. When everything seems like it's falling apart, nothing is working out for you. When you have nothing nice to say, its best to say nothing. When things are getting you down, nothing can pick you up. Do nothing, say nothing, feel nothing, think nothing and you will see nothing matters, a lot.

Why Bother?

Given how wonderful life can be, it's amazing how easy it is for things to bother us. The most bothersome things are often associated with the people we love the most. The people that are around us every day are always doing things that we think should not be done. Just as bad, they also don't do lots of things that we think should be done.

Parents constantly run into this problem with their children. It is the parents' job to teach children what they should and shouldn't do. When children do what they do and don't do, parents inevitably get annoyed.

Children constantly run into this problem with their parents too. While parents share their wisdom about what is to be done and not done, they themselves do or don't do things that can cause unbearable embarrassment.

While kids are busy bothering their parents, and parents are consumed with bothering their kids, kids are also bothering kids and parents are bothering parents. Sometimes this bothering is on purpose, sometimes it is by accident. When we are in the habit of being bothered, anything can become a bother. It could be a noise, gesture, word, facial expression, or smell. It could be somebody's absence or their presence. It could be the timing between their presence and absence. Trying to coordinate appearances and disappearances in time and space can be quite a bother.

If we decide we need to get a break from everybody around us, we may go for a walk. There, we the heat or cold, our path, our fellow walkers, their dogs, our dogs, the wind, the rain, or traffic could bother us. The world has an endless assortment of things to bother us, if we are predisposed to being bothered, which we are. Annoyance is certainly within our emotional range.

Why all the bother? Every little bother is life rubbing against us, like a purring kitten. The kitten is fully content, how we react is what concerns us. If we consistently recognize each bothersome event as a reminder to look for the love and life beyond the bother, we can use our pet peeves as opportunities to transform ourselves.

We can never learn to enjoy bothering, even though we know it is ultimately urging us along on our path, because if we enjoyed it, it would not be bothering. Also, we can never eliminate bothering. As long as we are there to be bothered, something will find us. We are left to embrace all the bother, to accept it as the friction of existence. Given how wonderful life can be, with parents, children, sun, wind, walks, dogs, kittens, transformation, and love, we can be bothered, and bother, to be mindful of our experience, live peacefully with each other, and bring harmony to the world.

Helping Others

The best way to help others is to forget about yourself. When you strive for enlightenment, the promise you make is to deliver all sentient beings from suffering. Then you begin your focused practice trying to become enlightened so that you are better able to help others. As you practice helping others you benefit immensely. As you try to bring peace to others, you feel peace. As you practice generosity and give to others, you feel wonderful. When you practice loving others, you feel joyful.

In order to help others, you have to help yourself. You can't help it. Helping others helps you. If you are too concerned about yourself though, you will have difficulty helping others. If you give to be thanked, you will not find satisfaction. If you love to be loved in return, you will often be frustrated. If you try to bring peace to others in order to pacify your own mind, that is still a good idea.

It is sometimes necessary to help yourself in order to help others. If you plan to help yourself now, so that you can better help others later, then you should practice compassion. Begin by practicing compassion for yourself, then widen the circle and practice feeling compassion for others. When you forget about yourself, you will be a great help to others. You will also feel peaceful, wonderful and joyful.

Other People's Minds

We spend so much of our time worrying about what is in somebody else's mind, but the real trick is reading our own minds. Other people will think what they will. We generally want them to like us. We may want them to love us, but regardless of how somebody else feels about us, how we feel about ourselves is what makes the difference. We may base how we feel about ourselves on how somebody else feels about us. That is totally normal. That is why it is normal to be totally crazy.

In order to combat total craziness, we need to take responsibility for our own feelings. If we decide we love somebody and then base our self worth on how they love us back, we are seriously entertaining the idea that we may not be worthy of love. We have decided that this other person is so wise, and their love is so valuable, that if they can't figure out just how to love us, then we are lacking that essential lovable quality. That's crazy.

We are completely lovable regardless of who notices it. Our self worth has nothing to do with who can see it. If we start to think that we are unlovable because of what we imagine is happening in somebody else's head, then our imagination is getting the better of us. If that happens, we're better off spending our time trying to read our own minds.

Crazy comes and goes. When we notice that we are entertaining thoughts that call into question our self worth, then we are entertaining craziness. If we think other people are better at judging our lovability than we are, then we are entertaining craziness. It's perfectly okay to entertain craziness, that's normal crazy. When we are able to see our craziness as it happens, we return to sanity. We know our self worth is immeasurable whether we, or anybody else, can see it.

When we find ourselves stuck worrying about what is happening in other people's minds, we can return to our own minds and remind ourselves that everything is fine. We are lovely, we are lovable, we are worthy. When we know that, other people, if they are at all aware, will notice it too.

Spiritual Envy

If you have ever listened to, or read, the words of a spiritual teacher and wished that you were able to understand life the way that person does, then you have experienced spiritual envy. Spiritual envy is the same as any other kind of envy, where it seems to you that another person has something that you lack. The feeling of envy is the same, but unlike envying a friend's new shoes, which you don't have, with spiritual envy, you actually have everything that the spiritual teacher has. You share the same spirit.

If you have a sense of spirituality that allows you to be inspired by spiritual teachers, then you have all the spirituality you need. That inspiration is you being in touch with your spirit. Feeling envy about the spiritual capabilities of the person who inspired you is overlooking the fact that the inspiration was in you. The teacher only evoked it, like a Parisian tour guide points out the Eiffel Tower.

If you ever notice yourself feeling spiritual envy, wishing that you could be enlightened like the Dalai Lama, remember, at that moment, you are filled with spirit. Enjoy your enlightenment.

Tea Party

If your fundamental Self of selves, your most basic nature, is the entire universe, including its awareness of itself, then your regular life is an illusion, a game of make believe, like a child's tea party. In order to live your life, you buy into that game with your soul.

Imagine you are a parent joining your child for a tea party. Your child, focused on the matter at hand, pretends to pour you a cup of tea. You sit at the little table with your child's stuffed bear and favorite doll and daintily sip a cup of air with your pinky extended. As a parent, you are thinking of other, more important, things you need to do, but there is nothing more important you could possibly do. Those more important things are the illusion. You joined the tea party filled with love and compassion for your child. The tea party is real.

When you suspect that your Self may be something other than a body trying to sustain itself in comfort and prestige, you still have to live among others in the illusion. All you can do is dress up in your fanciest hat, sit with the delightful company and enjoy the most delicious tea you can imagine.

Dream On

The nature of delusion is that it is convincing. It is tricky to become alert to your delusion. If you think that you might be awakening, how could you be sure that the awakening is not just a fancier layer of the delusion? What if what you experience is actually reality? If you are not deluded, but just living in reality, then there is no hope of awakening. Dream on.

Fortunately, we can tell the difference between delusion and reality. Sometimes, when we dream, we can tell within the dream that we are dreaming. The dream feels real, but we can recognize we are dreaming. Even if we don't notice we are dreaming when we are asleep, when we wake up, we know that we are back to reality.

In our reality, we can tell that most other people are kind of deluded. We know little kids are in their own world. The older generations also have their way of seeing the world. Every country in the world has a different view of how things are. People of different races, various sexual orientations, on different diets, and from the many religions all experience things from their unique perspectives. It seems so likely that our particular way of seeing the world will have an element of delusion to it. Yet that is reality.

Recognizing that you might be a little deluded gives you options. If you don't like the way you are feeling, you can console yourself with the idea that things are not exactly as they seem. If you feel sad, you can feel your sadness. You can feel the richness of the emotion, while understanding that beyond the sadness there is peace and joy. There is reality and there is delusion. There is sadness and there is joy. Such is our marvelous dream.

Life and Grief

The final stage of grief is acceptance. The first stage of grief is denial. Anger, bargaining and depression fall in the middle. Moving from denial to acceptance is the path of life. Nobody has to die to begin the grief process, we just have to be born. We are born with our Original Nature, which is inseparable from the universe. Our Original Nature is not concerned with life and death or good and bad, it is only concerned with being. As we grow, we learn to see ourselves as an independent body with its own name and separate existence. When we wholeheartedly believe that that is the way things are, we are immersed in stage one of the grief process, denial. In Buddhism, this is called ignorance.

When you experience your Original Nature, you recognize that you are connected to everything, from the beginning of time to the far reaches of space. That bag of blood and bones that was born and will die and seems to stand alone in the world is not the most pertinent part of you. There are logical ways to recognize this. Imagine your life without the sun and see that it sustains you as much as your heart does. To fully accept this, and move from a state of denial, requires that you experience your connectedness directly. In Buddhism, this is called enlightenment. Until you experience that, it's nice to imagine that it is there for you, whether you realize it or not.

In the stages of grief, between denial and acceptance there is anger, bargaining and depression. In Buddhism, those stages are called suffering. There is also happiness, joy, love, comfort and pleasure. These are not mentioned in the stages of grief, because they are not states that persist for long when you are grieving. In life, they occur in the midst of the suffering. If it were otherwise, nobody would survive long enough to recognize their Original Nature.

Through life, as we struggle with depression, anger and doubt, we can be patient with ourselves. As we wander through darkness, we engage our attention in all the concerns that seem far more pressing than realizing our Original Nature. Suffering is tiresome though. It is helpful to take a deep breath every now and again, listen to the soothing sounds of actual nature, feel the wind on our face and check in with our Original Nature. It's always right there for us, because it is us, more than we know.

As we observe our experience and practice accepting each emotion as it comes, we will learn to move quickly from denial to acceptance, from ignorance to wisdom. The intermittent stages of anger, depression, doubt, peace, joy and love will come and go quickly enough that they won't cloud our Original Nature with their residue. When we

are the sun, things burn up when we touch them
and we live in a blaze of glory.

Wondrous World

The world is an amazing place. The world is so wonderful that in order to survive in it, we have to train ourselves to ignore it. We have become so good at ignoring the wonderful things in the world that we can forget that the world is even a wonderful place. We may even imagine that it is a horrible place. When that happens we feel lousy, which confirms our suspicions about the world. With all the ignoring and imagining, we may miss what is real. To remind ourselves what is real, we have to stop thinking for a moment and just experience the wondrous world.

One of the most wonderful things about the world is the people. We surround ourselves with people that we love and then, in order to coexist with them, we ignore how much we love them. We focus on what we have to do. We notice things that annoy us. We think of ways that we wish these people would behave. Although we ignore the love, we know it is there. That can be frustrating and we may get upset because we are not experiencing the love the way we would like. Sometimes we even get mad at the Sun because it is too hot.

The good thing about all the ignoring we do is the world is still there. The love is still there when we're angry. The Sun is still out there at midnight. To experience the world's wondrous ways we just pay attention. It's all around us.

About the Author

On December 28, 2013, at the Awakened Meditation Centre in Toronto, Ontario, Canada, Zen master Bub-In, received Dharma transmission from his teacher and Zen master, Venerable Hwasun Yangil Sunim, who belongs to the Korean Jogye tradition.

Zen master Bub-In is also known as Peter Taylor. He practiced social work in Toronto for 10 years, where he experienced enough suffering to drive him to a serious meditation practice. He is the author of the blog, Zen Mister (zenmister.com). He currently lives in New Jersey with his wife and daughter.

About the Artist

In the same transmission ceremony, Zen master Hye-Chung received Dharma transmission from her teacher, Venerable Hwasun Yangil Sunim.

Zen master Hye-Chung is also known as Rebecca Nie. She is a professional artist based in Palo Alto California (www.rebexart.com).

About Inroads Press

Inroads Press (inroadspress.com) of Langley, WA is dedicated to promoting accessible and practical inroads into our personal capacities for healing and transformation.

Printed in Great Britain
by Amazon